JANE HARRISON is descended from the Muruwari people of NSW. Her first play, *Stolen*, had productions across Australia and toured internationally. She was co-winner of the 2012 RAKA Kate Challis Award for *Stolen*. *Rainbow's End* has had numerous productions since its premiere in 2003 and won the 2012 Drovers Award for best touring production. Both *Stolen* and *Rainbow's End* have been placed on secondary school curricula. *The Visitors* premiered at Sydney Festival in 2020. Her novel *Becoming Kirrali Lewis* won the 2014 Black & Write! Prize, and was shortlisted for the Prime Minister's Literary Awards and the Victorian Premier's Literary Awards.

Jane believes that stories have the power to reframe our national identity.

RAINBOW'S END

JANE HARRISON

CURRENCY PRESS
The performing arts publisher

CURRENCY PLAYS

First published in 2005
by Currency Press Pty Ltd,
Gadigal Land, PO Box 2287, Strawberry Hills, NSW, 2012, Australia
enquiries@currency.com.au
www.currency.com.au

This edition first published in 2023.

Cover design by Jenna Lee for Currency Press.

Currency Press acknowledges the Traditional Owners of the Country on which we live and work. We pay our respect to all Aboriginal and Torres Strait Islander Elders, past and present.

Contents

Lily Shearer and Phoebe Grainer in Darlinghurst Theatre Company's Rainbow's End, *2019 (Photo: Robert Catto)*

Introduction

As Aboriginal and Torres Strait Islander theatre makers our stories sit within a narrative framework defined by the concept of 'everywhen'.* What this means is that a story told today also may simultaneously exist in the past and will occur again in some form in the future. In other words, the past is the birthplace of our stories, the present is where our voice is heard, and the future is where our legacy is realised. Understanding that the stories of our people are told in this way is all about creating a sense of the world as it is, was, and always will be.

Similarly, Murrawarri playwright Jane Harrison has woven a sense of Indigenous temporality within her story *Rainbow's End*.

The characters in *Rainbow's End*, as historical fiction, are based on real life experiences of Aboriginal Elders in Victoria, from stories that were shared in interviews with Harrison. The three main characters in the play represent three generations of Aboriginal women existing in a single time. When we meet them they are living on a flood plain in a humpy on the fringes of a rural town. How each character responds to their circumstances tells us much about the Aboriginal women's experience of that time.

As with many similar texts, the play characters are introduced by way of a minimal outline that includes their age, sex, and relationship to other key roles. For example, Nan Dear (matriarch sixties), Gladys Banks (Nan's Daughter, Dolly's mother, forties), and Dolly (Glady's daughter, seventeen/eighteen). What makes these women Aboriginal is in the way Harrison guides us to a sense of their heritage as determined by their connection to country, the use of language terms, and their experiences as Aboriginal women. The men in the play however are transitory in thought and in action and add little to the overall story development.

---

*   The phrase 'everywhen' was coined by anthropologist
W E H Stanner to highlight an Indigenous concept of time unlike the
Western construction of linear time. *Everywhen* Ann McGrath, Laura
Rademaker and Jakelin Troy (Eds). UNSW Press 2023.

There is Errol the love interest, the Bank Manager, the inspector, the rent collector, the Jungi (Gun-gees) (police), and Papa Dear who never appears. It is worth pointing out that the Aboriginality of the women characters is not determined by the playwright.

In terms of the women's relationship to country the play is set somewhere near the towns of Shepperton and Mooroopna in Victoria on Yorta Yorta country near the banks of the Goulbourn River. However, this is not where the family originates from. Nan was born near the mighty Murray River that runs north of the Goulbourn River. In the play Nan tells us that her people were moved on from Cummeragunga, 'Our Home'. Historically, Cummeragunga was an Aboriginal mission near Brarimah in Northern Victoria and famous for the 1939 'walk off' of Aboriginal residents protesting the poor living conditions on the reserve. Nan carries this knowledge of her family's country and history with her. She also retains an understanding of her native tongue and tries to pass on this knowledge to her granddaughter Dolly. While working on their family history project Nan informs Dolly that their family tree is called a biyala or 'spirit tree'. Nan who a culturally informed woman with strong connections to her culture and history is the family Elder who lives in a type of survival mode that does not allow her to see beyond their current circumstances and therefore makes her sentimental about the past.

Nan's daughter, Gladys, on the other hand embraces the new and fantasises about a broader inclusive and equal society. She learns quickly however that her reality is a hidden one, swept out to the fringes of society, disregarded, and lacking in the most human of dignities. Her growing social and political awareness nurtures her aspirations for a better life than her current circumstances reflect. Gladys finds her voice in joining a local Aboriginal advancement league and speaking out publicly against the realities of Aboriginal life at that time. Although the play takes place in the 1950s, the character of Gladys seems to stand for the politically and socially aware and vocal Aboriginal woman of our current time. Women who have entered public life to advocate for the needs of their communities. Women like Malarndirri McCarthy, Nova Peris, Jacqui Lambie Mega Davis, Marcia Langton, Marion Scymgour, and Lynda Burney to name a few.

Finally, in *Rainbow's End* we have Dolly the daughter and granddaughter who is the educated hope for an enlightened future.

Since the 1994 Royal Commission into Aboriginal Deaths in Custody, education has been the priority and aspiration for many Aboriginal people. Importantly, there was an identified need for educating the broader population in Australia on the Aboriginal experience. In the play it is Dolly who educates the non-Aboriginal character Errol about her way of seeing the world, and the socio and political divide between black and white. Dolly as the emerging Elder is guided by her Elder grandmother. She is cognisant of the past whilst also aware of her present situation. In observing and supporting her mother's aspirations Dolly can also envisage a possible future for her family and people.

Although the play is set two generations ago, it is evident that we are currently living in this great era of change, and in continuing a discovery of our relationships and connections to the past, whilst living in the present the play *Rainbow's End* signals a possible beneficial future for the voice of Aboriginal Australia.

Liza-Mare Syron

Liza-Mare Syron is the Co-Founder and Senior Artistic Associate Moogahlin Performing Arts and Co-Associate Dean Indigenous. Faculty of Arts, Design and Architecture UNSW

Dalara Williams and Phoebe Grainer in Darlinghurst Theatre Company's Rainbow's End, *2019 (Photo: Robert Catto)*

Rainbow's End was first produced by Ilbijerri Theatre Cooperative at Bunjilaka, the Aboriginal Centre at Melbourne Museum, on Boon Wurrung and Woi Wurrung country, on 18 February 2005, with the following cast:

NAN DEAR	Beryl Booth
GLADYS	Pauline Whyman
DOLLY	Tammy Clarkson
ERROL FISHER	Gareth Ellis

Director, Wesley Enoch
Designer, Christina Smith
Lighting Designer, Marko Respondeck
Sound Designer, David Franzke

Acknowledgement

The author and publisher gratefully acknowledge permission to quote from 'Que Sera, Sera', words and music by Ray Evans and Jay Livingston. © St Angelo Music adm. by Universal Music Publishing Pty Ltd. © Jay Livingston Music. For Australia and New Zealand: Alfred Publishing (Australia) Pty Ltd (ABN 15 003 954 247), PO Box 2355, Taren Point, NSW 2229. International copyright secured. All rights reserved. Unauthorised representation is illegal. Reprinted with permission.

Writer's Note

Rainbow's End was commissioned by Ilbijerri Aboriginal and Torres Strait Islander Theatre Cooperative. The original brief was to tell a decade of Victorian Koori history and to write about 'the heroes'. There were many heroes in that era, but I was drawn to the 'unsung' heroes, and in particular the women who fought the good fight in their daily struggles to keep their families together, house, feed, clothe, educate, and above all, love and protect their children. (And aren't we all still fighting that good fight?) It's always a bitter-sweet experience researching the kinds of plays I'm drawn to write. Perhaps not bitter—a deep sadness for what our Elders had to suffer due to their Aboriginal heritage, sweet because of the poignant stories many of the Elders shared with me. Some of the Aunties that I spoke to recalled the freedom that they felt as children living on The Flats—that area between Shepparton and Mooroopna where many Aboriginal families lived on the fringe. They remember being protected from the reality of their often dire circumstances by their Elders—that was 'grown up business'.

I want to emphasise that *Rainbow's End* is a work of fiction—the characters and personal interactions portrayed are not based or real people or events, but I do hope they have an emotional truth. The exceptions are those historical events which backdrop the play, such as the Queen's visit and the development of the Rumbalara housing which occurred during the 1950s. I would like to express my sincere admiration to those families who lived on The Flats, and those who endured similar challenges, with thanks to all those who shared their stories. Thanks also to Ilbijerri and the fabulous and dedicated cast and crew who brought the story to life in its first production.

Jane Harrison
2006

CHARACTERS

Family on The Flats:

NAN DEAR, matriarch of the family, sixties

GLADYS BANKS, Nan's daughter, Dolly's mother, forties

DOLLY BANKS, Gladys's daughter, seventeen/eighteen

ERROL FISHER, whitefella, twentyish

Other characters, to be played by the actor playing ERROL FISHER:

BANK MANAGER

INSPECTOR

MR COODY, the RENT COLLECTOR

JUNGI, policeman

PAPA DEAR

VARIOUS OFFSTAGE VOICES (COUSIN, CROWD, COUNCILLORS, RADIO ANNOUNCERS, PRESENTERS)

SETTING

1950s. A humpy on the riverbank. Clean and homely.

Also: Daisch's Paddock (town tip); cork trees; BANK MANAGER's office; dance hall; new Rumbalara housing; and town hall.

ACT ONE

PROLOGUE: AFTERMATH

The song 'Que Sera, Sera' is heard.

SFX: Que sera, sera
Whatever will be will be,
The future's not ours to see
Que sera, sera.

It's late spring, late afternoon and gloomy outside. Inside their humpy NAN DEAR *and* GLADYS *are rebuilding after a flood has devastated their home. Everything below three feet is sodden and mud splattered.* GLADYS *mops, wrings out, and removes things that are destroyed.* NAN DEAR *finishes hanging a piece of hessian to replace a ruined piece that lined the interior walls. Now she covers the hessian with pages from a magazine.*

NAN DEAR: *[pointing to some magazines]* Pass those.
GLADYS: They're Dolly's.
NAN DEAR: They're dry.

> GLADYS *hands them over and* NAN DEAR *rips the pages, slowly and deliberately, pastes them with homemade glue and sticks them, upside down, onto the hessian. After a time* DOLLY *arrives home from school and surveys the scene critically. She toes the old, ruined lino. She sighs, resigned. Until she spots her magazines. She goes to protest, sighs again, resigned.* GLADYS *fakes cheerfulness.*

GLADYS: It'll be all right.
DOLLY: You always say that.

> NAN DEAR *and* GLADYS *take a quick look at each other.* NAN DEAR *gestures for* DOLLY *to come over. She does, and* NAN DEAR *gives her granddaughter a hug.*

> *The lights go down.*

SCENE ONE (A): THE QUEEN'S VISIT

Humpy interior. Morning. GLADYS *is getting dressed up and humming to herself.* DOLLY *has her head down over her schoolbooks.*

GLADYS *listens in rapt silence to the voice of Queen Elizabeth II on the radio.*

THE QUEEN: [*voiceover*] … standing at last on Australian soil, on this spot, which is the birthplace of the nation, I want to tell you all, how happy I am to be amongst you, and how much I look forward to my journey amongst Australia …

> *The radio fades out as* NAN DEAR *enters.*

GLADYS: That valve … Where's my white gloves?

NAN DEAR: Gloves? Don't need white gloves to pick beans.

> GLADYS *doesn't react.*

You're going into town then, for all that hullabaloo. Think of inviting me?

GLADYS: You? I know how you feel about royalty. Even if she is the 'first reigning monarch to visit our shores'.

DOLLY: Nan, I need your help with this.

> *She is doing homework.*

NAN DEAR: One loyal subject in the family is enough. And someone's got to pick.

DOLLY: I'm doing our family tree.

NAN DEAR: Tree?

GLADYS: Don't know about loyal. Just going for a squiz.

NAN DEAR: Don't know where you get these ideas from sometimes.

GLADYS: I'm not hurting anyone, am I? It's a moment I'll remember … to see our pretty young monarch and the Duke. I'm not going to miss it for all the tea in China!

> GLADYS *flounces out to the back room.*

DOLLY: Nan?

NAN DEAR: [*to herself*] Tree? [*To* DOLLY] You mean the biyala? Spirit tree, branches hanging low over the river?

DOLLY: Like this.

> NAN DEAR *looks over* DOLLY*'s shoulder to see the diagram she is making.*

I need to list all our family members ... our parents and their parents and so on ...

> NAN DEAR *picks up a pencil and begins to write over* DOLLY*'s shoulder.*

... but not cousins.

> NAN *stops writing.*

NAN DEAR: And why not cousins? What kind of a fool thing ... ? You need to know who your cousins are. So you don't marry 'em.

> GLADYS *returns.*

GLADYS: Queen Victoria married her cousin—'Prince Albert of Saxe-Coburg'.

NAN DEAR: Well, we don't.

DOLLY: [*baiting her*] And Mum told me that 'our lovely young monarch', married her Greek/German cousin, Prince Philip—

GLADYS: My glory, it was a beautiful wedding—

NAN DEAR: Hmmp. No good'll come of it. Their children will be retarded, or, or worse, funny in the head.

> *Beat.*

GLADYS: Could you listen out for the taxi?

NAN DEAR: [*incredulously*] The taxi?

GLADYS: It's Aunty's shoes. I don't want Her Majesty to see them dirty.

> NAN DEAR *just shakes her head in disgust.* DOLLY *giggles, then stops as* NAN DEAR *glares at her.* GLADYS *gets money out of the jam tins for the taxi.*

DOLLY: I gotta put down where you were born, Nan.

NAN DEAR: My birth certificate says 'Murray River'. Born there and, by crikey, I'm gunna go back and die there.

DOLLY: Nan, you're not gunna die. You're gunna live for ever.

NAN DEAR: Well, of course I'm not gunna die. Not here, anyway. Gotta go back to me old place to do that. And I'll have a feed of—

DOLLY: Swan eggs.

NAN DEAR: [*threateningly*] Deary me, that girl mustn't want help with her homework …

> DOLLY *looks contrite.*

Swan eggs, before I go.

DOLLY: [*to herself*] Mother, Gladys Banks. Grandmother, Alice Louise Cooper. Nan, if you love that Murray River so much, why don't you still live there?

NAN DEAR: [*bitterly, half to herself*] They forced us to leave. Forced us to leave Cummeragunja. Our home.

DOLLY: Who, Nan? Who did?

> *But* NAN *doesn't want to talk about that business and* DOLLY *knows it. She goes back to her homework.*

Grandmother, Alice Cooper who married Reginald Harold Dear. Reginald Harold Dear's parents are … Nan?

NAN DEAR: Is that your taxi, Gladys? [*Cagily*] I don't keep details like that in me head.

DOLLY: [*to herself*] You do so.

> GLADYS *rushes over to the window.*

My great grandparents, Nan …

GLADYS: No …

DOLLY: Nan?

NAN DEAR: [*to* GLADYS] You'd better wait on the track. Else the taxi will pick up one of the cork-tree lads. [*Dryly*] I'm sure they'll want to celebrate the Queen's visit.

GLADYS: Oo, I hadn't thought of that … How do I look?

DOLLY: Fit for a queen!

> GLADYS *is pleased by the compliment but pretends not to show it.*
>
> *The lights change to a dream sequence:* GLADYS, *curtsying, is presenting a bouquet of flowers to the* QUEEN. *Instead of being formal, the* QUEEN *pulls her into a hug.*
>
> *The lights come back to reality.* GLADYS *is holding a bunch of weeds. She looks at them as if she can't understand why she is holding them. She waves goodbye and leaves.*

[*Dismayed*] So it's buka bung stew tonight!

NAN DEAR: If I don't get on that truck and do an honest day's work, it will be. And you, off to school.

DOLLY: But I haven't finished—

NAN DEAR: Quick … go. But keep away from them cork trees.

DOLLY: Yes, Nan. You've told me a hundred times.

NAN DEAR: Don't be cheeky.

DOLLY: Yes, Nan.

NAN DEAR: Good girl.

DOLLY: Yes, Nan.

> DOLLY *exits.*
>
> *The lights indicate a time change.*

SCENE ONE (B)

The radio is heard featuring a description of the Queen's 1954 Royal Tour of Australia.

ANNOUNCER: [*voiceover*] In every town it was something different. In Shepparton, it was babies. My word, babies everywhere! All washed and dress and fit to meet the band. No wonder the Duke called out, 'Where's Father?'

> GLADYS, *holding a very wilted bunch of flowers, comes inside the humpy and plonks down in the only chair. She kicks off her shoes.* DOLLY *watches her.* NAN DEAR *is cooking.*

GLADYS: Oh, my feet! Remind me never to borrow Aunty's shoes again.

NAN DEAR: What about the taxi?

GLADYS: Didn't show, did it? So I walked up to the causeway—

NAN DEAR: That's not far.

GLADYS: Then all the way to Shepp.

NAN DEAR: To Shepp? Why?

GLADYS: On account of the hessian.

NAN DEAR: What hessian?

GLADYS: The hessian they lined the road with. The hessian that I couldn't get through and couldn't even peek over.

DOLLY: What they do that for?

GLADYS: Stop the likes of her seeing our humpies.

NAN DEAR: Dolly, bring the wood in.

DOLLY *sighs and exits.*

GLADYS: If they'd given us better houses … But hessian! Like a band-aid over a sore—

NAN DEAR: What are they going to do with all that hessian?

GLADYS: Oh, Mum, doesn't it bother you?

NAN DEAR: What good is it if I get het up? My job is to get food on the table—

GLADYS: But decent housing, Mum—

NAN DEAR: Gladys, get off your high horse. Least here we do things our way—no one breathin' down our necks. Not like those last days at Cummeragunja.

> *Beat.*

Anyway, it's Papa Dear's mission to make things better for the Aboriginal people.

> *Beat.*

Papa Dear had a meetin' with her, you know.

GLADYS: Our head of state? He had a meeting? With our queen?

NAN DEAR: She's not my queen. But yes, that's how important—

GLADYS: —he is.

NAN DEAR: —she is—getting a meeting with the busiest Aboriginal around!

GLADYS: Why didn't you tell me?

NAN DEAR: I just did. He popped in to see us. But you were out gallivanting.

GLADYS: I missed him … ? Did he say what she was like?

NAN DEAR: For goodness' sake!

DOLLY *returns and is listening with interest.*

GLADYS: And I was just hoping for a glimpse.

DOLLY: Did you get one?

GLADYS: No …

NAN DEAR: Gawd, daught, where do you get these highfalutin' ideas from?

GLADYS: Well, it's either from you, or it's from Papa Dear, and somehow I don't think it's from—

NAN DEAR: Don't just sit there, girl. Stoke the fire.

DOLLY: Yes, Nan.

GLADYS: Yes, Mum.

The radio fades up again.

ANNOUNCER: [*voiceover*] And just to remind the royal couple that they were in Australia, we showed them how to throw a boomerang … It really does come back …

The lights go down.

SCENE TWO (A): OH, ERROL

As the lights come up, GLADYS *is chopping wood with an axe and listening to Bob Dyer's quiz show,* Pick-A-Box, *on the radio.*

BOB DYER: [*radio voiceover*] With what is the tail of the beaver covered?

GLADYS: [*to herself*] The answer to that'd be scales.

CONTESTANT: [*radio voiceover*] Fur?

She pauses, waiting for the answer.

BOB DYER: [*radio voiceover*] I'm sorry, it's scales! An unusual bit of nature there.

GLADYS: 'Course.

She resumes chopping.

BOB DYER: [*radio voiceover*] What is the more common term for an ocular contusion?

NAN *appears, carrying two dead rabbits.*

GLADYS: A black eye.

NAN DEAR: Whose black eye? You mean, Ester's—

GLADYS: Shh!

NAN DEAR: [*to herself*] Oh, that.

She gives the radio a dirty look.

Thought you were talkin' sense for once.

NAN *starts to skin the rabbits.*

CONTESTANT: [*radio voiceover*] A swollen eye? A damaged eye?

Pause.

BOB DYER: [*radio voiceover*] Yes! That's good enough! I was debating that for a moment! You were quite correct, medically. But, to put it bluntly, the more down-to-earth one is …

GLADYS *and* BOB DYER: [*simultaneously*] … a black eye.

> DOLLY *steps outside the humpy, throws out the tea leaves from the billy, and pauses. She is chewing gum.*

DOLLY: Who's got a black eye?

NAN DEAR: Doesn't concern you, Dolly.

> NAN DEAR *turns the station on the radio.* GLADYS *goes back to her chopping.*

DOLLY: You should go on *Pick-A-Box*, Mum, you're ace.

NAN DEAR: A black contestant? I'd like to see that!

DOLLY: How could they tell?

> *She has a sly look at* NAN DEAR, *then flicks the radio back to* Pick-A-Box.

BOB DYER: [*radio voiceover*] Our next contestant is petite and lovely. Who is she?

> *A female voice on the radio is heard giggling.*

> NAN *looks at* DOLLY *who turns the radio off.*

DOLLY: [*dreamily*] One of the boxes has a real mink stole, from the House of Biba. I could see you picking up that prize, eh, Mum?

NAN DEAR: A mink stole around here?

GLADYS: And why not, Mum? It gets cold at night here, too.

NAN DEAR: Just not going to happen. Not in my lifetime.

DOLLY: I bet there's a lot of things that you couldn't have imagined, Nan. Bodgies and widgies, canned food—

NAN DEAR: That's been around. Saved our skins many a time.

DOLLY: —the hokey-pokey …

> *She dances around.*

I'll teach you, Nan.

NAN DEAR: Can't teach an old dog new tricks.

DOLLY: [*dreamily*] Maybe Mum will surprise you …

> *The lights change for a dream sequence.*

The radio crackles to life.

BOB DYER: [*radio voiceover*] Howdy, customers. We're in the third week of our Melbourne season …

DOLLY: [*radio voiceover*] And our latest contestant is Mrs Gladys Banks from Moo—roo—

GLADYS: That's Mooroopna.

BOB DYER: [*radio voiceover*] Just to recap … You won two prizes, didn't you? A sewing machine that does everything under the sun— overlocking, buttonholes, embroidery stitches—and a mink stole!

DOLLY: [*radio voiceover*] From the House of Biba, Gladys …

The scene fades out as the lights fade back to reality.

DOLLY: Mum'll be on the radio, she'll win all those wonderful prizes, she'll be a hero—

GLADYS: [*correcting her*] Heroine.

NAN DEAR: Why you don't listen to Jack Davey, Gladys. At least he's Australian, not one of them flash Yanks.

DOLLY: Get with the times, Nan, this is the fifties!

NAN *turns her full attention to* DOLLY.

NAN DEAR: I've heard you were talking to Leon Arnold.

DOLLY: So?

NAN DEAR: [*threateningly*] Speak cheek to me … Where were you talking?

DOLLY: Just … along the track …

NAN DEAR: He's your uncle's cousin.

DOLLY: I'm not marrying the boy. [*Learned by rote*] After all, I can't marry an Arnold, can't marry an Anderson, can't marry a Brock.

GLADYS: You can't marry anyone—

DOLLY: —they're all related—

GLADYS: —least not till you've finished your studies. And get a good job. In town—

DOLLY: By then I'll be old. How old were you, Nan?

Her chewing-gum bubble pops.

NAN DEAR: Just get the water.

DOLLY: Yes, Nan.

NAN DEAR: And don't let that boy get fresh. He's got a wild look.

DOLLY: No, Nan.

NAN DEAR: [*to herself*] Motherless child, poor lad …
GLADYS: And practise your French verbs.
DOLLY: Oui, Madame.
NAN DEAR *and* GLADYS: [*simultaneously*] Good girl!

> DOLLY *pushes an old pram, which holds a kero tin, in the direction of the river. They watch her depart, then both sigh.*

NAN DEAR: French verbs! Mink stoles! You put ideas into that girl's head.
GLADYS: She needs to know the world is bigger than just this.
NAN DEAR: She doesn't need to know any more than she does.

> *Beat. She is holding up a rabbit.*

I'm taking this over to Ester's. Seems they're in a bit of a spot. She's with child again …
GLADYS: Oh, I didn't know—
NAN DEAR: … and she woke up with an [*mimicking* BOB DYER] ocular contusion … from that whitefella husband of hers.
GLADYS: I hadn't heard.
NAN DEAR: If you spent less time on them quiz shows, you'd know more.
GLADYS: Yes, Mum.

> NAN DEAR *exits with rabbit in hand.*

SCENE TWO (B)

The lights come up on DOLLY *pushing the pram, while a Brylcreemed lad,* ERROL FISHER, *wobbles up on a bicycle from the opposite direction. He nearly falls off his bike at the sight of her.*

ERROL: Morning, miss.

> DOLLY *nods and* ERROL *checks out the contents of the pram as he passes. Once they have passed each other they look back and check each other out—an instant spark of attraction passing between them.* DOLLY *exits.*

> ERROL *dismounts and studies his map. He looks puzzled, but puts the map away and pushes on towards* GLADYS, *who is still chopping wood.*

> ERROL *pulls out a heavy book from the pannier on his bike and*

takes a tentative step towards GLADYS.

Excuse me, sir …

She stands there with the axe.

GLADYS: Yes? Can I help you, lad?

ERROL: Sorry, er, ma'am. [*Extremely nervously*] My name is Errol Fisher. I am a representative of … er … I am in this area today, with quite an amazing offer. Um … I have a presentation regarding …

He offers the book. GLADYS *looks at it with interest.*

As you can see … it is that most famous of tomes, the—

DOLLY *has returned and at the sight of her* ERROL *clumsily drops the book.* GLADYS *picks it up …*

DOLLY: I don't think so, mister. They're not for the likes of us.

… and dusts it off tenderly. She hands it back to him.

ERROL: [*defeatedly*] Rightio.

ERROL *turns his bike around.*

GLADYS: Wait. [*To* DOLLY] Haven't you got a job to do?

ERROL *turns back, a glimmer of hope.* DOLLY *puts her nose in the air and exits.*

[*To* ERROL] What did you say that was?

ERROL: It is …

Celestial music is heard for a moment.

… the *Encyclopedia Britannica*! If I could be permitted to demonstrate its points, its, um, say … say …

GLADYS: Salient?

ERROL: Yes, salient points … Rather, if I could just—at least—run through my, you know … Well, I would truly appreciate it—

GLADYS: Sit down, son.

ERROL *notices* GLADYS *is sitting on a kero tin so he does the same.*

ERROL: Presenting … the *Encyclopedia Britannica*. Your entrée to the world of learning, a world of discovery, a world of fascinating facts …

GLADYS *flicks through the book with interest.*

GLADYS: Like on *Pick-A-Box*?

ERROL:YES! One of last year's contestants read the *Britannica* for half
    an hour each night, and attributed that to the secret of his, his, um …
GLADYS: Success?
ERROL: Yes! His success!
GLADYS: Only half an hour?
ERROL: But that's not the end of it! Madam, do you have children?
GLADYS: Yeah, four of 'em. All grown up and working, except Dolly,
    she's my youngest. You know, Bob Dyer's wife's name is Dolly. You
    saw her just then—my Dolly, not Bob Dyer's Dolly.
ERROL: That was your daughter? And you're her …
GLADYS: Yes. [*With pride*] Her mother. Mrs Banks.
ERROL: Mrs Banks.

    Beat.

Where were we? Yes—for keen fans of *Pick-A-Box*, there's nothing
    like the *Britannica* … er … Children—you have four … um …
GLADYS: But only one at home, the boys are all away shearing.
ERROL: Yes … because it is for school-aged children … [*Nodding in*
    DOLLY*'s direction*] She's … ?
GLADYS: School-aged. Nearly seventeen.
ERROL: Ah! … that this encyclopedia set is most beneficial. It will open
    up a world of dis …
GLADYS: Discovery.
ERROL: Discovery … set them up on a lifelong love of learning, help with
    school assignments, allowing them to reach their full potential …

    The lights change for a dream sequence. GLADYS *sees* DOLLY *in*
    a robe and clapboard hat.

GLADYS: [*to herself*] My girl, a graduate …

    The lighting fades back to reality. GLADYS *looks around, fearful*
    that her 'daydream' has been witnessed, but it hasn't. NAN *returns.*
    ERROL *rises politely.*

ERROL: Ma'am.
NAN DEAR: [*hissing to* GLADYS*, jutting her lips in* ERROL*'s direction*]
    What's he doing here? He's not the Welfare?
GLADYS: No.

NAN DEAR: Churchy type? Tell him we only got time for Papa Dear. He's our pastor.

GLADYS: The lad's doing a presentation.

NAN DEAR: A what?

GLADYS: Mum.

>   *And she's dismissed. Glowering,* NAN *tends the fire.*

You were saying? Set them up? Just one book will do all that?

ERROL: Not one, ma'am. Twenty-four!

GLADYS: [*faintly*] Twenty-four?

ERROL: You've seen the condensed version. Now imagine your own leather-bound library in the environment of your own home …

>   *They are lost in their thoughts.*

GLADYS: Set them up for life, you reckon?

ERROL: Er, it appears that at this point in time, I am expected to … Well, it's here that I get out the sales order form …

>   NAN *hovers.*

NAN DEAR: [*to* GLADYS] Ask him what it says in that there encyclops about the Aborigines, eh?

GLADYS: Now, Mum.

>   ERROL *timidly flicks through the volume.*

ERROL: Er … um … it says, that … Well, I'm quite sure there's a full and very enlightening entry in the complete set.

NAN DEAR: [*to* GLADYS] Is he just?

GLADYS: Mum!

ERROL: So, Mrs, er … Banks … if you're interested, we can fill in your details …

>   *He hands a fountain pen and the order form over to* GLADYS. *She freezes momentarily.* DOLLY *returns unnoticed.*

GLADYS: Now where have I placed my glasses … ?

>   NAN *springs into action.*

NAN DEAR: Neglected to tell you, love, I stood on 'em. Earlier. All smashed.

ERROL: That's terrible!

DOLLY *stands over* ERROL.

DOLLY: You made a wrong turn somewhere. Hand over your map.

ERROL: [*worriedly*] It's the company's! If I misplace it they will dock my pay tuppence.

DOLLY: You got an encyclopedia, so how come you know nothing, eh?

ERROL: Er …

DOLLY: As Nan would say, you really came down with the last shower, didn't you? Hand it over.

ERROL: Yes, miss.

DOLLY: Here's where you went wrong. You turned onto this track, whereas you should have headed over this way and not crossed over the railway line. Here's where all the toffs live. The whitefellas in their fancy new homes that Mum reckons they think is too good for blackfellas. Shoulda known when you come across blackfella housing that you'd missed your turn-off. You must have a lousy sense of direction.

ERROL: Yes, miss.

GLADYS *stands up and picks up the axe.*

GLADYS: Yes, son, you'd better ride on over there. That's where you'll be selling your encyclopedias. Not here.

The other two nod in agreement.

ERROL: Yes, ma'am. I'll just leave my calling card. I'll write my name on it. Just in case, ma'am.

GLADYS: Don't get called that too often—ma'am.

She laughs.

Just in case!

ERROL: Yes, ma'am. Thank you, ma'am.

GLADYS: Dolly, show the young man the track. Point him in the right direction.

DOLLY *and* ERROL *move off.* NAN *rushes over to* GLADYS.

NAN DEAR: [*hissing*] Call her back. Right now.

GLADYS: He's an [*with awe*] encyclopedia representative, Mum.

NAN DEAR: Think I don't know a snake-oil salesman when I see one!

GLADYS: He seems nice. Real polite. And she needs to talk to people who are doing something with their lives. People with important jobs, not just picking, like us.

NAN DEAR: We only pick 'cause that's all they'll let us do.

GLADYS: Exactly.

> NAN *is watching* DOLLY *and* ERROL *suspiciously from the window.*

NAN DEAR: Anyway, he smells of perfume. What kind of fella smells of perfume?

> GLADYS *starts singing 'I've Got the World on a String'. She is looking at* ERROL*'s card.* NAN *notices.*

Now, Gladys, you won't be needing any of them encyclops. Won't help you answer any more questions on the *Colgate Palmolive Pick-A-Box*, will it?

GLADYS: Yes, Mum. No, Mum.

NAN DEAR: That's right! So don't go getting ideas. Hardly got two pennies to rub together.

> GLADYS *continues to sing softly, as the spotlight goes on* DOLLY *and* ERROL.

DOLLY: Sold many?

ERROL: Um … This is my first presentation. Well, the first one I got all the way through, anyhow.

DOLLY: Fair dinkum?

ERROL: You see, I just got in. The company gave me a map and a bicycle and a train ticket to Mooro—Moo—roo—

DOLLY: Mooroopna.

ERROL: Thanks. I've never been so far from Melbourne.

DOLLY: So you're from the big smoke? What's it like?

ERROL: Good, I suppose. Just like anywhere.

> *He looks around.*

There's picture theatres and municipal pools—

DOLLY: They have them here too, you know …

> *Except they're segregated. She moves away from him.*

You go the way I told ya. On the other side of the railway line. You'll sell plenty of them encyclopedias there. Fancy coming to The Flats!

ERROL: Yes. But all's well that ends well.

DOLLY *looks at him, puzzled. He couldn't possible mean her, could he?*

I get to deliver them. In four weeks … [*Shyly*] Will you be around in four weeks, when I make my deliveries?

DOLLY: 'Spose. Not going anywhere.

He goes to put the book in the bicycle pannier but his bike is not there. A bicycle bell is heard offstage.

Not delivering them on ya bicycle, I hope?

ERROL: No … the company utility. Where is my bicycle?

DOLLY *whistles extremely loudly.*

DOLLY: [*in a loud blackfella accent*] Oi! You little monkeys, get that ruddy bicycle back 'ere, or I'll give youse a kick up the moom! [*Politely*] And you were worried about losing your map!

The sound of the bicycle being dropped offstage.

There it is. Well … goodbye, then.

ERROL: Goodbye, then … and thanks.

DOLLY: What for?

He stands and watches her while she returns to the humpy.

The lights go down then come up on the interior.

As DOLLY *enters,* GLADYS *puts down* ERROL'S *business card with a sigh, but remains transfixed by it.*

GLADYS: You're right, Mum.

DOLLY: What is she right about?

NAN DEAR: She's the cat's mother. And I'm right about everything.

NAN *begins stoking up the fire.*

DOLLY: [*chuckling*] He sure got a fright when his pushbike wasn't there.

GLADYS: Ester's boys took it for a spin?

DOLLY: Their legs could hardly reach the pedals. Lionel on the handlebars. Roy on the back and Robbie on the seat! Lad didn't seem to understand what a novelty a new Malvern Star is around here.

NAN DEAR: Come here, darling.

DOLLY *dutifully goes over and gives* NAN *a hug.*

You watch who you're mixing with. Hard to tell a good man from a bad. Bad one will promise you everything, then do the straight opposite, just like that.

> NAN *snaps her fingers and* DOLLY *repeats the gesture.* GLADYS *just rolls her eyes.*

GLADYS: You get back to your books, Doll.

> GLADYS *looks at the card again.*

DOLLY: But I need an encyclops to do me homework!

> DOLLY *squeals in mock horror as* NAN *chases her around inside the humpy with a wooden spoon.*

GLADYS: Do you? [*To herself*] No … Silly woman.

> *But she puts the business card down the front of her dress.*
>
> *The lights go down.*

Lily Shearer, Dalara Williams, Phoebe Grainer and Lincoln Vickery in Darlinghurst Theatre Company's Rainbow's End, *2019 (Photo: Robert Catto)*

SCENE THREE: LINO

DOLLY *is rummaging at the town tip. She looks at, and discards, a few items.*

The lights change to a dream sequence. A well-groomed SALESMAN *appears.*

SALESMAN: [*poshly*] May I be of assistance, miss?

DOLLY: [*poshly*] Why yars, I'm after new linoleum.

SALESMAN: We have a wide selection.

DOLLY: This pattern.

SALESMAN: Exquisite! Thank you for shopping at Daish's once more.

> *The lights change back to reality.*

> DOLLY *hoists the lino roll over her shoulder as the* SALESMAN *fades away.* DOLLY *walks past the cork trees. She sees someone in the shadows.*

COUSIN: [*offstage, slurring*] Hey, Dolores. You look real pretty today.

DOLLY: Hey, Leon.

COUSIN: [*offstage*] Why don't yah join us? We're having a bit of a party … You look like a party girl.

DOLLY: Nah, I'm busy. Nan's expecting me.

COUSIN: [*offstage*] 'Nother time then, Dolores.

DOLLY: Yeah, sure.

COUSIN: [*offstage*] Promise?

DOLLY: 'Course, cuz.

> *As* DOLLY *staggers along* NAN *appears, going in the opposite direction.*

NAN DEAR: Good girl! [*Suspiciously*] Which way did you come?

DOLLY: Aren't you just glad I found it?

NAN DEAR: Yes … If I catch you going past those cork trees—

DOLLY: In good nick and all.

NAN DEAR: —mark my words, I'll wallop you.

DOLLY: Nan, I'm nearly seventeen. You can't scare me with 'boogey man' stories any more. And besides, them goomees are harmless.

NAN DEAR: What you call them? Shame! They might be drinkers, but they're still our people.

DOLLY: [*to herself*] And model citizens to boot.

NAN DEAR: Show some respect, girl. They've had it hard, those lads.

DOLLY: How, Nan?

NAN DEAR: Never mind. They just have.

DOLLY: [*with a sigh*] Yes, Nan.

> *Beat.*

Where's Mum?

NAN DEAR: Cannery. Wrangled another shift.

DOLLY: Why? What's she saving for?

NAN DEAR: Grown-up business.

DOLLY: Where you off to?

NAN DEAR: Spud Lane.

DOLLY: No need to ask what's for tea, then.

> NAN *exits and* DOLLY *staggers on, but when she sees* ERROL *leaning against the humpy wall, his bicycle nearby, she dumps the lino.*

It's you.

ERROL: I came to see your mother. About the encyclopedias.

DOLLY: Oh? Oh! But she won't be home for a bit.

ERROL: Really? I'll just have to wait. [*He planned it that way.*] It's a beautiful day.

DOLLY: It's stinking.

ERROL: It is hot … out here.

> *He eyes the humpy, but* DOLLY *won't acquiesce.*

You've been at school?

DOLLY: You ask a lot of questions.

ERROL: My dad reckons I ask too many. But now it's part of my job. They train me to ask questions.

DOLLY: Really?

ERROL: Do you mind if … ?

DOLLY: Another question?

ERROL: May I have a glass of water?

> *He wipes his brow.* DOLLY *hesitates, then nods. He goes as if to enter.*

DOLLY: You can't come in … The … um … baby's sleeping.

ERROL: [*alarmed*] Baby? It's not … ?

DOLLY: It's … it's my cousin's baby.

> *She goes in and quickly returns, barefoot, with a cup of water.* ERROL *looks at the tin cup with interest.*

ERROL: It's made out of a can!

> DOLLY *is humiliated but* ERROL *doesn't notice.*

How do you do that? You people can make something out of nothing.

> *He sees her reaction too late.*

I, ah, I mean, I'm not trying to … to …

DOLLY: [*bitterly*] 'You people'?

ERROL: I didn't mean … crikey Moses … It's fascinating.

> *Beat.*

Is it a little girl?

DOLLY: Pardon?

ERROL: The baby.

DOLLY: Oh, ah, ye—Ah, no, a boy.

> *She softens at his interest.*

ERROL: Would you like to go for a ride?

> *She is uncertain but hops on the bike. It wasn't what he had in mind … he was thinking for a dink. She rides around in a figure-eight and he trots to keep up with her. She starts to hum a popular song and after a while he joins in with the words.*

DOLLY: [*shyly*] Is it good selling encyclopedias?

ERROL: Sure. I'm out and about—free. I meet all sorts of people. What about you? What will you do when you leave school?

DOLLY: Pick.

ERROL: Pick?

DOLLY: You know, fruit … Or the Blue Moon.

> ERROL *is puzzled.*

The cannery.

> *Beat.*

Maybe the hospital …

ERROL: Hospital?

DOLLY: Well, who knows … ?

ERROL: You should come to the city. There's swags of work. And you'd like the city.

DOLLY: Would I? Nan wouldn't like that. City's are full of sin.

ERROL *laughs.*

Anyway, what would I do?

ERROL: [*boldly*] What do you want to do? A girl like you … you could do anything you want.

DOLLY: You sound like my mum.

ERROL: She must be smart.

DOLLY *shrugs, both proud and embarrassed.*

DOLLY: She's …

ERROL: What?

DOLLY: Never mind.

Beat.

I'd like to be a model, like in the magazines, or an actress, like Gina Lollobrigida … She's so … so … well, you know … [sexy …] But really, I … it's silly, but I'd kind of like to be a nurse.

She's dreamy.

ERROL: That's not silly … Nurse Dolly.

DOLLY: But Mum reckons I'm good with figures—you know, algebra. Of course you know. But what could I do with that?

ERROL: Why, lots—

But he doesn't get a chance to tell her, as GLADYS *appears with a crappy old bookcase balanced on the old pram.* ERROL *leaps over to help her.*

GLADYS: [*loudly*] We'll be needing one of these, eh, Errol?

ERROL *holds his finger up to his mouth.*

ERROL: Baby's asleep.

GLADYS: Baby?

DOLLY: [*firmly*] Cousin's baby.

GLADYS *nods, a little puzzled. She pats the bookcase.*

GLADYS: Good old Daish's. Actually, I thought I saw you on the other side, Dolly.

ERROL: Daish's?

DOLLY: [*warning her*] Mum.

GLADYS: It's the tip.

> DOLLY *shoots her a glare but* GLADYS *has a head of steam and keeps going.*

It should have been where they built us housing, being the highest land around here … but, oh no, they decided to turn it into the town tip … [*uncertainly*] actually.

> *They watch* DOLLY *go inside, humiliated.*

I'm sorry. You don't need to hear—

ERROL: It's okay.

> *They are both embarrassed.* ERROL *turns his attention to the bookcase.*

Just needs a lick of paint.

GLADYS: That's what I thought.

> *Triumphantly she pulls an obviously used and bashed can from the pram.* GLADYS *laughs and* ERROL *joins in.*

> *The lights go down.*

SCENE FOUR: HOUSE OF BIBA

GLADYS *serves out the stew while* DOLLY *sets the table.*

NAN DEAR: You haven't set a spot for Papa Dear.

DOLLY: What's the point?

NAN DEAR: Just do it.

DOLLY: It's been three months.

NAN DEAR: He's busy doing good work. God's work and hard work.

GLADYS: I heard he's in Western Australia. Touring the communities there. Doll, did you see that photograph that he sent over? It was in the newspaper and all.

> *Beat.*

He could walk through that door any day now.

The lights change for a dream sequence. PAPA DEAR, *in old-fashioned hat and coat, dances in, throws his hat on the hatstand, kisses* GLADYS *on the top of the head, and dances out. No-one takes any notice of him but* GLADYS, *who smiles at him warmly.*

Papa Dear …

DOLLY: Okay, okay … an empty place for Papa Dear. [*To herself*] Just as well he likes potatoes.

She sets another place and they begin to eat.

[*To* NAN] Potato stew tonight, Nan? What a surprise!

NAN DEAR: [*warning her*] Cheeky …

DOLLY: Mum, there's a summer job going at Trevaks that I could try for. They teach you the cash register. And I could maybe get offcuts for you to sew, Nan! I know I could do it.

GLADYS: Of course you could!

NAN DEAR: You'll be at the Blue Moon. With us. As usual.

GLADYS: [*hopefully*] But it sounds like a good job … a good opportunity …

But NAN *will brook no argument. She shakes her head and that's that.*

NAN DEAR: It's a bit chilly tonight, go get me a cardie, Doll.

DOLLY *leaves the room. As soon as she's out of sight,* NAN *hisses at* GLADYS.

They're never going to give her that job.

GLADYS: She's good with figures.

NAN DEAR: A girl from The Flats? I don't even see the town Aboriginals working in stores.

GLADYS: Why should her address stop her in life?

NAN DEAR: Gladys, get a grip.

GLADYS: [*to herself*] I'm trying, Mum, I'm trying.

Hurt, she turns the radio on. DOLLY *returns with the cardigan that she puts around* NAN'S *shoulders.*

DOLLY: [*radio voiceover*] … only Ajax with the miracle foaming action cleans so quick, works so easily and polishes so bright.

BOB DYER: [*radio voiceover*] You sound like one of the elves in the commercial. Very good. Cleans so easy …

NAN DEAR: Elves, cash registers ... That's exactly what I'm talking about.

> *She looks at* GLADYS *accusingly.*

SCENE FIVE: THE DELIVERY

Interior of the humpy.

DOLLY *and* ERROL *look slightly more mature than their earlier scene together.* DOLLY *is really embarrassed that* GLADYS *has allowed* ERROL *into the humpy.*

DOLLY: [*whispering*] But why do you have to do it in here?

GLADYS: It's ready to storm out there ... Volume A would get wet.

> GLADYS *turns her attention to a brown-paper parcel.* NAN *is holding back. Throughout, she is openly hostile to* ERROL.

Cuppa, Errol?

ERROL: Actually, I'd love a cup of coffee if you've got one, Mrs Banks. But, first, don't you want to see it, in all its glory?

GLADYS: Coffee? Coffee, you say?

> *She gestures for* DOLLY *to come closer, whispering.*

Dolly, nick next door to Uncle's and see if he has a jar of coffee. Hurry up. [*To* ERROL] Coffee won't be a moment, lad. Oh, and it nearly slipped my mind, the down payment. We'd better sort that out first. Dolly, get down the jam tins, will you please?

> DOLLY *passes* GLADYS *the jam tins, one at a time.*

Now. Pear money, peach-picking money, tomatoes—hardly anything in that tin, not worth picking them at tuppence for ten pound. Only bonus is they give you the bruised ones.

> DOLLY *glares at* GLADYS *who is oblivious.*

NAN DEAR: The bruised ones that otherwise go to the pigs.

> GLADYS *carefully empties each tin and counts up the coins. (She knows exactly how much is in each tin.)* DOLLY *hands* GLADYS *the last of the jars.*

GLADYS: Not that jar, Dolly, that's your glory-box stash.

> DOLLY *looks embarrassed. She exits.*

Orange money—don't like picking them, don't like getting up them ladders one bit.

NAN DEAR: At least you're clear of the snakes up there.

ERROL: Snakes?

GLADYS: Always snakes in paddocks. Once when Dolly was a babe in a wooden box, tea towel over her to keep off the sun—and come smoko I went to feed her and there was this massive carpet snake curled up with her! And my Dolly was fast asleep! Not a peep out of her! She was a good baby.

ERROL: And it didn't bite her or anything?

They look at him askance.

NAN DEAR: [*to herself*] It was a mamel.

GLADYS: A carpet snake, love.

ERROL *doesn't comprehend.* DOLLY *returns and busies herself making the hot drinks.*

ERROL: Oh? But you killed it anyway?

NAN DEAR: [*to herself*] Killed it! Encyclops boy and he knows nothing!

DOLLY *sniggers.*

GLADYS: They keep down the mice. Anyway … two pounds six shillings deposit. Six shillings every three months for twenty-four months, that's the deal.

DOLLY: Oh, and here's the contract all filled in.

She hands the contract to ERROL *who scans it.*

ERROL: And signed by you, Mrs Banks?

GLADYS: Done!

ERROL *looks slightly puzzled, but then gets excited.*

ERROL: Done! Not my first sale, but surely my longest negotiation. Six months! Now … drum roll please …

GLADYS: Oh, I'm so excited!

He hands over the parcel and GLADYS *tears it open. She opens the book—celestial music is heard. She touches the pages lovingly, then holds the book out for* DOLLY. DOLLY *has to first hand* GLADYS *and* ERROL *their cuppas.*

Isn't it … extraordinary … daught? Volume A! Would you look at the pictures? In colour too! Coffee okay, son?

ERROL takes a quick sip and nearly gags.

ERROL: Just lovely, ma'am.

NAN DEAR just scowls. GLADYS *puts Volume A pride of place in the middle of her new bookcase.*

GLADYS: Call me Aunty, Errol. I imagine we'll be seeing a bit of you.

She looks from ERROL *to* DOLLY *and back again.* DOLLY *looks embarrassed.* NAN *scowls even more.*

When he comes to pick up the payments.

NAN DEAR: You mean you've got to pay more for those things?

The lights go down, then come straight up again.

DOLLY, *outside the humpy, is leaning against the wall, while* ERROL *fumbles with his keys.*

ERROL: Miss Banks …

DOLLY: Dolly. We're not too fussed about fancy titles.

ERROL: Dolly …

DOLLY: Yes?

ERROL: Dolly … That's a pretty name.

DOLLY: It's Dolores, actually.

ERROL: Really? That's pretty too …

DOLLY moves away slightly, and ERROL *quickly speaks to hold her attention. But she was only getting a piece of wattle gum to chew.*

Um … Do you like music? Oh, I'm sure you do. [*Curiously*] What's that?

DOLLY: Snooty goggles.

She gives him a piece to chew.

ERROL: Snooty … ?

DOLLY: Goggles.

ERROL: Hmmm …

DOLLY: If you don't like it …

ERROL: But it's interesting.

GLADYS *opens the door and sweeps some dirt outside, studiously ignoring the young 'ens.*

[*Nervously*] Er … I was thinking … Dolores …

GLADYS *makes encouraging motions at him.*

DOLLY: Really?
ERROL: Yes.

ERROL *looks sideways at* GLADYS, *who pointedly goes back inside.*

Why do you live out here?
DOLLY: Where else would we live?
ERROL: In town?
DOLLY: Nan likes to be near all the other families. And Mum does too but—
ERROL: The other families …?
DOLLY: You ask a lot of questions. Can't you find the answers in there?

She points to the encyclopedia.

ERROL: [*grinning*] Not the answers to the questions I want to ask. Like …
DOLLY: Yes?
ERROL: Like … [*In a rush*] There's a dance on in Shepparton next Saturday …
DOLLY: True?
ERROL: There is. With a band playing … a good band …
DOLLY: How do you know that? You seen 'em? You heard 'em?
ERROL: No, actually.

Pause.

You do like music?
DOLLY: Already told you that.
ERROL: 'Cause I was thinking …
DOLLY: You were thinking …
ERROL: If I organised my schedule … Well, funnily enough, I already have, and I was thinking …
DOLLY: Yes, thinking …
ERROL: Which means I happen to be in Shepparton on Saturday. Which means …
DOLLY: It means … ?

ERROL: That I'm available ... and if you're available ...

DOLLY: Available ...

ERROL: And interested ...

DOLLY: Yes ... yes ... go on ...

ERROL: Well, I'd be most pleased if you would—

> GLADYS *bursts out of the humpy.*

GLADYS: Oh, for heaven's sake, spit it out, will ya, son?! [*To* DOLLY] He wants to invite you to the dance.

DOLLY: Mum!

ERROL: Mrs Banks!

NAN DEAR: [*from inside, loudly*] Glaaadys!

> GLADYS *hurries inside.* DOLLY *moves up very close to* ERROL'*s face.*

ERROL: So will you? Will you go with me?

DOLLY: Listen, fella. Do you have any idea what'll happen if you walk into that dance with me?

ERROL: Uh, no ... [*Worriedly*] Is there some other bloke on the scene? Is that it? Will some fella want to punch me on the nose for sweet-talking his girl?

DOLLY: You're white. I'm Aboriginal. Or haven't you noticed?

ERROL: Well, yes ... but ...

DOLLY: I'm from The Flats. Not even one of those townie types of cross-over Aboriginals.

ERROL: What matters is you. Not your address ...

DOLLY: That's sweet.

> DOLLY *visibly softens towards him.*

NAN DEAR: [*from inside, yelling*] Dolly!

DOLLY: Go! You'll get us in trouble.

ERROL: Who with?

> DOLLY *starts to move away but he grabs her hands and slowly they move into a jitterbug, dancing perfectly together. We hear the song 'A Girl Like You' by Cliff Richard and the Shadows.*

You're going to come with me, then?

> DOLLY *knows their relationship cannot work.*

DOLLY: No ... it's ... impossible.

But he pulls her back towards him.

ERROL: Nothing's impossible. Can I pick you up from here?

She shakes her head.

Then I'll meet you halfway.

DOLLY: With your sense of direction?

ERROL: There's these gnarled trees down the track.

DOLLY: The cork trees.

ERROL: All twisty and rough.

DOLLY: I know them.

ERROL: That can be our special meeting spot!

DOLLY: I'm not sure.

ERROL: It's here—or it's there. What'll it be?

DOLLY *hesitates.*

DOLLY: I'll meet you at the hall.

ERROL: And I'll bring you home? Swell.

DOLLY: Swell.

He swings her away ... There is a sound of the door being opened, and DOLLY *swings out of his reach.*

NAN DEAR *appears and the music stops suddenly, as if the record has been scratched, and the mood is broken.*

DOLLY *goes in without a word.* NAN DEAR *looks daggers at* ERROL.

NAN DEAR: It's getting dark. Very dark. Time for you to move on. Take the short cut, past the cork trees.

She moves inside and slams the door.

The lights fade.

SCENE SIX: THE INSPECTION

NAN DEAR *and* GLADYS *are inside the humpy, straightening everything in sight with a nervous, anxious energy.*

NAN DEAR: [*whispering*] I'm worried about Ester.

GLADYS: Send Doll over.

The two women stand up—as if at attention—as the INSPECTOR, *a well-dressed white man, steps back into the front room.*

INSPECTOR: I say, crocheted pillow shams. Such beautiful work!

GLADYS: That would be my mother's handiwork.

INSPECTOR: And your name is … ?

GLADYS: Mrs Banks.

INSPECTOR: And … ?

GLADYS: My mother, Mrs Dear.

> *The* INSPECTOR *is writing notes.*

INSPECTOR: [*pleasant, but distracted*] Is there a Mr Banks?

GLADYS: Deceased. He fought in the war.

INSPECTOR: Is there a Mr Dear?

GLADYS: Yes, Papa Dear.

INSPECTOR: And he is where, at present? At work?

GLADYS: Why, yes. In the Western District, I believe.

INSPECTOR: Away shearing?

NAN DEAR: He's a pastor. Our own pastor.

INSPECTOR: Pastor Dear? I do believe I have heard of him. He does good works among your community.

NAN DEAR: Yes.

GLADYS: He's very well-known …

> *But he's moved across the room and* GLADYS *is unsure whether to continue that line of conversation.*

INSPECTOR: It must be quite unpleasant here in summer?

GLADYS: Excuse me?

INSPECTOR: The heat.

GLADYS: It's bearable. Better than winter.

INSPECTOR: Oh?

GLADYS: Because of the floods.

INSPECTOR: How frequently does it flood?

GLADYS: [*unsure*] Oh, now and then. Now and then.

INSPECTOR: So, only the two back rooms … Are there children staying with you?

GLADYS: My children are all grown up, off working—

> *At that moment* DOLLY *bursts in, as if she has something urgent to say.* NAN DEAR *is gesticulating for* DOLLY *to shoo.*

NAN DEAR: [*whispering*] Give Ester a hand.

But DOLLY *has been spotted.*

GLADYS: Except for my daughter.

The INSPECTOR *appraises* DOLLY.

INSPECTOR: And she is … ?

GLADYS: Dolores. Dolores Alice Banks. She's just back from the high school. She's currently undertaking her [*with a hint of triumph*] Leaving Certificate.

For the first time he turns his full attention to the women.

INSPECTOR: Really? That's the way! And what does the future hold for you, Dolores?

DOLLY: Well, I'd like to work at the hospital—

GLADYS: —as a bookkeeper—

NAN DEAR: —in the laundry.

The INSPECTOR *is not sure if they're having a go at him or not. He notices the floor.*

INSPECTOR: Linoleum?

NAN DEAR: Yes.

GLADYS: From Daish's.

INSPECTOR: I'm not familiar with the department stores around these parts.

DOLLY *has to put her hand over her mouth to suppress a giggle. The* INSPECTOR *looks out the humpy window. He clasps his hands together, his 'tour' completed.*

Well! I don't know how you do it. Your whites are so white! With river water, no less!

GLADYS: Just boiled up in a kero tin, with Velvet soap and a blue bag, same as everyone.

INSPECTOR: Yes … As a result of my report, things will change, Mrs Banks. Things must change. The sanitation arrangements for one.

GLADYS *and* NAN DEAR *exchange worried looks.*

And you need interim housing to ease you into the townships. Are you aware of the concept of assimilation, Mrs Banks?

GLADYS *isn't sure how to respond, or even if a response is required.*

GLADYS: Yes, but we—

But NAN DEAR *elbows her.*

INSPECTOR: The Aborigine needs to be absorbed into the community. But how can he be absorbed until he learns to live like us? I will recommend assimilation, in my report. It is a vexed issue, to be sure, but someone must take leadership. First, the housing problem must be fixed … After all, how can the children study in the evenings if there is no electric light?

GLADYS: [*unsure*] Yes.

INSPECTOR: Yes. I will do all I can. But … in the meantime, you need to rally yourselves. Speak to your local MPs. Form a delegation. Collect petitions. Write letters. Inform yourself. Knowledge is power, ladies.

GLADYS: [*hesitantly*] Yes. [*More assured*] Yes.

INSPECTOR: Thank you for the cuppa, Mrs Dear. Mmm … something smells delicious?

NAN DEAR: It's just damper.

GLADYS: Please help yourself.

INSPECTOR: Marvellous! Quite a treat, fresh damper. Thank you.

NAN DEAR: Yes.

GLADYS: Do come again.

> NAN DEAR *elbows* GLADYS. *The* INSPECTOR *exits.* GLADYS *rubs where* NAN DEAR *elbowed her.*

NAN DEAR: [*disgusted*] 'Do come again!'

GLADYS: My Lordy, I was nervous.

DOLLY: What is he here for? Why is he checking us out? And who is he?

NAN DEAR: Never you mind.

> *She is peeking out the window, checking out which way he is going.*

DOLLY: Nan, why do you always treat me like a child?

GLADYS: [*low*] That man, he's writing a report. About the way we live. For the Government of Victoria.

DOLLY: A report? Like a mark out of one hundred?

GLADYS: Something like that.

DOLLY: Will they build us our own houses, like you're always on about?

GLADYS: Perhaps.

> NAN DEAR *snorts.*

DOLLY: Do you still want me to go over to Aunty Ester's?

NAN DEAR: [*sadly*] Probably too late now.

> *Beat.*

DOLLY: Nan? What's wrong, Nan?

> NAN DEAR *shakes her head and vanishes outside to hide the anxiety she is feeling.* GLADYS *watches* DOLLY *watching her.*

GLADYS: [*falsely bright*] So how was school today, Dolly?

DOLLY: Same as every day … Mum! Nancy was talking about a ball that's coming up. The Miss Mooroopna-Shepparton Ball! Mum?

> GLADYS *has not been listening.* NAN DEAR *returns and shakes her head at* GLADYS*'s inquiring look.*

GLADYS: Well then, Dolly—haven't you got sums to do?

DOLLY: Yeah, so I can be a bookkeeper … in the laundry.

> DOLLY *scoots out of reach but* NAN *doesn't even try to smack her. The two older women look at each other, then in the direction* DOLLY *has gone, worried.*

Phoebe Grainer and Dalara Williams in Darlinghurst Theatre Company's Rainbow's End, *2019 (Photo: Robert Catto)*

GLADYS: They won't take her.

NAN DEAR: She's seventeen. They'd make her work for someone. Like they did you.

GLADYS: I think he was impressed at her schooling.

NAN DEAR: Maybe. And how clean it was?

GLADYS: Definitely. Oh, Mum … But I'd like to see that report of his—I'd like to know what he says about us.

NAN DEAR: [*an outburst*] And what bloody good would that do?! Daydreams!

Crankily, she thumps the radio to life.

GLADYS: [*to herself*] They're not really daydreams …

Because she intends to make them come true.

SCENE SEVEN: THE TURN

Early evening.

DOLLY, *out of sight, is singing to the radio.* NAN DEAR *sits in the only chair, cleaning a pair of slingback shoes with white shoe cleaner. She is acutely aware of what is happening around her.* GLADYS *is fussing around getting ready, and also singing—but a different song.*

GLADYS: My white gloves?

NAN DEAR: Tomato box by the bed.

GLADYS: You need a cuppa, Mum? [*Louder*] Get a wriggle on, Dolly.

NAN DEAR: Full up to pussy's bow.

DOLLY: Where's the talcum powder?

NAN DEAR: Trough.

DOLLY: Thanks, Nan. Can I use a little of your lavender water? Thanks. You got your glasses, Nan?

NAN DEAR: Right here, love.

GLADYS: Mum, you sure you don't want to come to Aunty's? Did I mention it's a housing fundraiser?

NAN DEAR: You did. Why else would you make rock cakes all afternoon?

GLADYS: Just six dozen. It's my little contribution. See, Uncle's planning to negotiate for Daish's, in a 'new deal'. They've got in mind Aboriginal housing. They want to call the housing Rumbalara. It means—

NAN DEAR: I know what it means.

GLADYS: —'end of the rainbow'. Sounds beaut, doesn't it, this 'new deal'? They say the houses'll have running water …

The lights change for GLADYS*'s dream sequence.*

A tap appears from nowhere and from it flows blue jewels in an approximation of water. NAN DEAR*'s words break in and bring the fantasy to an end as the lights change back to reality.*

NAN DEAR: But Daish's is the town tip. They already decided that in '47.

GLADYS: He's—we're—going to have another go at it. I might even go on the committee.

NAN DEAR: You? Don't ever get too clever, my girl.

GLADYS: Just a thought.

NAN DEAR: You get knocked down when you get too clever.

GLADYS: Yes, Mum. I'll get you comfy with the radio.

She fiddles with the radio.

RADIO ANNOUNCER: [*voiceover*] Ajax foaming cleaner. Because Ajax contains bleach, you'll stop paying the elbow tax …

NAN DEAR: Honestly, they're mad about whiteness.

GLADYS *belts the radio and it reverts to soothing country and western music.*

GLADYS: You got your crochet hook, Mum?

NAN DEAR: Stop fussing.

GLADYS: Dolly, would you like to borrow the girdle? That dress—

DOLLY *walks in, looking gorgeous in a very tight-waisted 1950s dress.*

NAN DEAR: —that dress never looked like that on you.

GLADYS: A vision! My baby …

She twirls DOLLY *around, proud as.*

NAN DEAR: She doesn't look like a baby.

GLADYS: I'm off now, Mum, unless there's anything … ?

NAN DEAR *shoos her away.*

You look beautiful, Dolores. Truly beautiful. [*Whispering*] Have a lovely time … with Errol.

GLADYS *gives* DOLLY *a peck on the cheek and exits.* NAN DEAR, *once she's gone, rushes over and gets the latest volume of the encyclopedia to look at. She settles back in her chair and notices that* DOLLY *is still there.*

NAN DEAR: Aren't you going with her?

DOLLY: [*evasively*] Ah, no. I'm getting a lift. On account of Aunty's shoes.

DOLLY *puts on earrings and fiddles with her hair.*

NAN DEAR: [*suspiciously*] All this fuss for a little bush concert?

DOLLY: I'm not going to the fundraiser.

NAN DEAR: You're not? Then where, pray tell?

DOLLY: To a dance. In Shepparton.

NAN DEAR: Your mother know this? Of course—she's in on it. Who's going to be at this dance?

DOLLY: The usual.

NAN DEAR: Who's bringing you home? One of your cousins? At least Gladys would have made sure you were brought home safe.

DOLLY: Errol's bringing me home.

NAN DEAR: That encyclops boy? That gubba fella?

DOLLY: Mm-mm. Errol Fisher.

NAN DEAR: He's Errol Fisher? A Fisher?

DOLLY *sighs.*

He'll be there?

DOLLY: Everyone's going to be there! It's a dance, Nan.

NAN DEAR *goes into a coughing fit. As* DOLLY *rushes to get her a glass of water,* NAN DEAR *hides the white shoes.*

You right, Nan?

NAN DEAR: I'm chilly.

DOLLY *gets* NAN *a blanket and arranges it over her knees.*

You get going, then … My crochet hook?

DOLLY: I'm sure you had it … Here it is! Nan, have you seen those shoes?

NAN DEAR: Aren't they under Glad's bed?

DOLLY *disappears then reappears shaking her head.*

DOLLY: [*panicking*] What time is it?

DOLLY *finds the shoes under the chair. There's a truck honking outside and* DOLLY *rushes to the window.* NAN DEAR *coughs again.* DOLLY *'s concerned.*

NAN DEAR: Parched … But you'd better be off … Go out, kick up your heels, love … Don't mind me here all alone.

DOLLY *fills up her mug from the billy.*

DOLLY: You sure?

NAN DEAR: Though I do feel like a serve of swan eggs …

DOLLY: Swan eggs? You're okay, aren't you, Nan?

NAN DEAR *coughs.* DOLLY *looks from the source of the honking to* NAN DEAR. *The honking is more insistent. The coughing is more wracking.* DOLLY *opens the door and disappears.*

NAN DEAR *rushes over to the window, then rushes back and settles herself back in her chair. As* DOLLY *returns inside (waving sadly to the departing truck)* NAN DEAR *looks relieved, then remembers to cough again.*

NAN DEAR: Come here, love.

DOLLY *dutifully goes over and gives* NAN DEAR *a hug.* DOLLY *removes her accessories.* NAN DEAR *perks up.*

DOLLY: Okay now, Nan?

NAN DEAR: So, so.

DOLLY *strokes* NAN DEAR*'s hair tenderly.*

Perhaps I will go to the concert, a little later on. A few hymns would be lovely. You can walk me over, Dolly. There'll be a few young 'ens there. Heard there's a nice Wemba Wemba boy down from Swan Hill …

DOLLY *hugs her, disappointed in missing the dance.*

DOLLY: We're probably related to him too, eh, Nan?

NAN DEAR: We'll find someone for you. Go on, put on your earrings, love.

The lights go down.

SCENE EIGHT: WASHING-DAY BLUES

As the lights come up, NAN DEAR *is wringing out the whites, then hanging them on the old-fashioned clothes line (no pegs).* DOLLY, *dragging her feet as she walks home from school, wordlessly plonks down her bag and gives her a hand.*

DOLLY: Nan, Robbie wasn't at school today. Neither was Lionel or Roy.
NAN DEAR: Yes.
DOLLY: It's 'cause of that inspector, ay, Nan?
NAN DEAR: [*harshly*] Don't listen to gossip, Dolores.
DOLLY: Is that why Aunty Ester's down at the cork trees, drinkin' with the goo—?
NAN DEAR: Don't speak ill, girl.
DOLLY: But is it 'cause they took her boys?

> NAN DEAR *shoots her a look of warning.*

I want to know. I'm not a child. I'm a woman, Nan.

> NAN DEAR *will not answer.* DOLLY *turns on the radio.*

RADIO ANNOUNCER: [*voiceover*] And in other news, well-known Melbourne vocalist and teenage idol of thousands, Ernie Sigley, will sing with the Echuca Rhythm Kings orchestra at the inaugural Miss Mooroopna-Shepparton Ball. So, girls, put on your prettiest frocks, and be there … And now here's Lucky Lennie's …
DOLLY: The Miss Mooroopna-Shepparton Ball …

> *There's longing in her voice.* NAN DEAR *goes to get another load of washing from the kero tin.* GLADYS *hurries up the track towards them.*

GLADYS: Dolly! There's a trainee program, at the bank, in town. I heard Nancy Woolthorpe's mother talking about it when I was at the butcher's.
NAN DEAR: When you're the last to be served, you hear lots of things.
DOLLY: And?
GLADYS: And? You'll go for it. If Nancy's going for it, you can.

DOLLY: What do you want from me, Mum? Do you want me to walk like them, talk like them, wear a twin-set like them? Pretend to be one of them?

GLADYS: Are you finished?

DOLLY: No. And yet we live like this … out here.

NAN DEAR: At least here we sink or swim on our own. Not like the Cummeragunja days, always at the mercy of the manager—

She stops abruptly, a little shamed by her outburst. DOLLY *is pleased that* NAN DEAR *has revealed a little info. But* GLADYS *has something to say.*

GLADYS: You ask me what I want. Well, I want what any mother, black, white or brindle, wants for her daughter. That's all.

GLADYS *stares at them defiantly, before she goes into the humpy.*

DOLLY: Nan … why don't we have a normal life?

NAN DEAR: This is normal—

DOLLY: Getting flooded all the time—

NAN DEAR: It's just the way it is. That's nature.

DOLLY: But why? It's like we're fighting nature all the time. Living on the riverbank—

NAN DEAR: You're the one who's fighting. You and your mother. Fighting against how things are.

DOLLY: What's wrong with that? Papa Dear fights for things to get better.

DOLLY *sighs, resigned. They continue to hang up the washing.*

It's not going to rain, is it?

NAN DEAR: Would I be doing this if it was about to rain?

Beat.

All these questions, questions, questions …

DOLLY: Yes, Nan. But how come there's no answers?

Beat.

NAN DEAR: A ball.

DOLLY *is surprised that* NAN DEAR *has revived the topic.*

DOLLY: Not just any ball. The Miss Mooroopna-Shepparton Ball.

NAN DEAR: Is it just for Aboriginals?

DOLLY: No.

NAN DEAR: That boy's not going to be there? That encyclops boy?

DOLLY: Doubt it …

> *She waits, then buries her face in a white sheet.*

'Your whites are so white, Mrs Dear.'

NAN DEAR: As if that were the be-all and end-all. As if that were the bloody be-all and end-all.

> *Beat.*

All right.

DOLLY: All right, what?

NAN DEAR: You can go.

DOLLY: I can? To the ball? And enter the competition? Yipee! You'll make me a new dress, Nan? A really gorgeous one with lots of fabric—pretty fabric.

NAN DEAR: Maybe.

DOLLY: Please, Nan.

NAN DEAR: Yes. Yes.

> DOLLY *dances around* NAN DEAR.

Haven't you got something to do instead of getting under people's feet, girl?

DOLLY: I could get the water?

NAN DEAR: You go and play. While you're still a child. Git.

DOLLY: Thanks, Nan. A big skirt. And a peplum.

NAN: Peplum?

DOLLY: Like in the picture on the wall. Love you, Nan.

> DOLLY *hugs her.*

NAN DEAR: Don't get your hopes up. It's not the House of Biba, you know. Go on, git.

> *The lights go down.*

SCENE NINE: HOME SWEET HOME

As the lights come up, GLADYS *is going around the humpy emptying the mouse traps of dead mice and setting new traps, while* DOLLY *does her homework. A song is heard on the radiogram: 'I'll Be Home' by Pat Boone.*

GLADYS: First hint of cold weather and they're in, like a flash.

> DOLLY *sings a line from the song.*

I made another payment today.

> DOLLY *glances up and sees another volume of the encyclopedia is on the bookcase.*

DOLLY: Up to K. I'll be nineteen by the time we're up to Z.

> DOLLY *goes over and gets down the latest volume and pours over it.*

GLADYS: You do think they're wonderful, though? You're 'expanding your possibilities'?

DOLLY: Of course, Mum. Every day I learn something new about the big, wide world. That see-through section with the body—the muscles, and the bones, and the veins—that's my favourite. I love reading about the gizzards.

GLADYS: My … gizzards. That makes it all worthwhile.

DOLLY: [*casually*] So you saw …

GLADYS: [*equally casual*] He inquired after you.

DOLLY: He did?

> GLADYS *picks up a mouse that is still alive.*

GLADYS: I'll let this one go in the scrub.

DOLLY: So it can just find its way back here?

> GLADYS *vanishes outside with the mouse and* DOLLY, *restless, checks out her reflection in a small cracked piece of mirror.* GLADYS *returns.*

[*Casually*] Errol … ?

GLADYS: Oh, yes, he was sorry he missed you the other week. He happened to ask if you were attending this ball coming up. And I said, yes, by coincidence, you were!

DOLLY: So what else did he say?

GLADYS: He asked if he could meet you at your 'special spot'. Asked. Real polite. Now, don't mind Nan—it'll be our little secret. What she won't know—

DOLLY: —won't hurt her. Except—Nan already said I could go. She's making me a dress. With a peplum.

> *She points to a picture of a peplum on the wall.*

GLADYS: [*annoyed*] Did she just? And why was it her place to give you permission?

DOLLY: Mum!

GLADYS: Well, it's not right. I'm the mother.

DOLLY: Yes, [*exaggerating*] Mum. [*Dreamily*] So we ren-des-vous [*rhyming with booze*]—

GLADYS: If you spent more time on your French, and less time staring at peplums, you'd know it's pronounced 'rendezvous'.

DOLLY: [*angrily*] You think you know everything—

GLADYS: I don't—

DOLLY: Too right, you don't.

GLADYS: [*quietly*] Don't speak to me like that.

DOLLY: You going to wash out my mouth with soap? Nan thinks soap and water, and you think that books and school, are the answer to everything.

GLADYS: You're not too old for a wattle stick across your bare legs.

DOLLY: You've never hit me in your life.

> DOLLY *and* GLADYS *are locked in a staring match.*

It's me that gets stones thrown at her when I walk down the street. It's me that gets snide remarks.

GLADYS: You think I haven't had my fair share? Or Nan? Even Papa Dear—not even he escapes it. Don't think he doesn't get put in his place.

> *Beat.*

You have to learn not to let them shame you.

DOLLY: Have you, Mum? Have you learnt not to be shamed by them?

> *Beat.*

I thought not. You're always telling me to stick up for myself, but when do you, eh?

> *A long pause.* DOLLY *exits.* NAN DEAR *enters.* GLADYS *vents her frustration.*

GLADYS: [*angrily*] Re this ball, why are you saying if she can step out? She's my daughter. I have brought up three others before her.

NAN DEAR: Boys, Gladys. Girls are a different kettle of fish.

> *Beat.*

GLADYS: I'll make the decisions regarding Dolores, thank you.

NAN DEAR: Then do it.

GLADYS: I have. She's going to the ball. And Errol Fisher is walking her home.

NAN DEAR: But—

GLADYS: No.

> NAN DEAR *goes to protest further but holds her tongue when she sees the look on* GLADYS*'s face.*

SCENE TEN: THE BANK VS MRS BANKS

The interior of a BANK MANAGER*'s office.*

GLADYS, *who's all dressed up, is sitting in the visitor's seat while the* BANK MANAGER *sits behind his desk.*

BANK MANAGER: And how can I be of service, Mrs … ?

GLADYS: Banks. Mrs Len Banks.

BANK MANAGER: Mrs Banks. You're inquiring about a loan, perhaps?

GLADYS: Oh, no. It's about my youngest, Dolly.

> GLADYS *rummages in her bag.*

BANK MANAGER: And she … ?

GLADYS: Pardon?

> *She triumphantly produces a photo of* DOLLY. *The* BANK MANAGER *puts on his glasses and studies the photo.*

BANK MANAGER: Yes. Very pretty face.

> *Beat.*

But I'm still not sure why you're here …

GLADYS: The teller's position, of course.

BANK MANAGER: I don't think so …

GLADYS: But she's just completed her Leaving Certificate—the first in the family—with real good grades … 'N' top of her class in algebra …

> *Her earnest dialogue is hardly heard as we hear* DOLLY, *who becomes visible behind the gauze, picking fruit in an orchard and singing the chorus of 'Catch a Falling Star'.*

> *On the* BANK MANAGER*'s desk is a tray with two china cups of tea, milk jug and sugar bowl. He pours a cup for himself, but*

doesn't offer one to GLADYS. *As the song ends, and the image behind the gauze fades, we return to* GLADYS*'s words.*

... She'd be a fine asset. Here's her school report—see, all As and Bs—and she won this for best and fairest for women's basketball ...

She hands over the report and a ribbon.

BANK MANAGER: Well, it's all very impressive ... What I'm wondering is how she'd fit in.

GLADYS: [*steely*] She'd fit in fine.

BANK MANAGER: In a job such as this, reliability is important ... I wondering how would she get into town each day.

GLADYS: She has a bicycle. She's on time for school. Look ...

She pulls out of her bag a special certificate for punctuality.

For punctuality.

BANK MANAGER: Splendid. Now, rapport with our customers is important—sorry, rapport means—

GLADYS: [*through gritted teeth*] —getting along. Making people feel comfortable, like.

BANK MANAGER: Yes.

Beat.

Mrs Banks, are you a customer of this bank?

GLADYS: Well, no. [*Confessing*] I've never even been in one of these before.

BANK MANAGER: A Bank Manager's office?

GLADYS: A bank!

BANK MANAGER: But everyone needs savings ...

From his drawer, he produces a tin money bank and a passbook and hands them over to GLADYS.

You put your pennies in here, when they add up to a pound, you bring them in to us and we write the amount in your savings book. It helps you to save for something special, and you know that your money is safe.

GLADYS: Just like jam tins.

BANK MANAGER: Just like jam tins.

GLADYS *looks at the tin then, seeing the* BANK MANAGER'*s gesture, she gets out her purse. He indicates to her that payment is not needed and she puts the tin in her bag. They both smile weakly.*

Well, if that's all …

He stands up, as if their business has concluded.

DOLLY: [*voiceover echo*] Have you learnt not to be shamed by them? Eh?
GLADYS: No. The trainee position. For my Dolly.
BANK MANAGER: To be honest, Mrs Banks—
GLADYS: She'd be an asset. She's a hard worker. She knows all about hard work. She's honest. She's polite. She deserves a break. One little break. Are you going to be the one to offer her that break, sir?

She stares him down. He taps his fingers together for what seems like an eternity.

BANK MANAGER: Why not?

Beat.

Please add her name and address to this list …

He hands her a clipboard. She takes it.

… and she'll be notified of an interview time.

GLADYS *shakes her head.*

Oh! I beg your pardon.

He hands her his fountain pen. She holds it, uncertain, then hands it back. She collects her things as if to leave.

Mrs Banks?

Beat.

Oh, fountain pens are a little tricky, aren't they?

He calmly begins to fill out the form and GLADYS *sits back down.*

Your daughter's full name, Mrs Banks?
GLADYS: Dolores. Dolores Alice Banks.

The lights go down.

SCENE ELEVEN: THE BALL

The sound of big-band swing music is heard.

When the lights come up, DOLLY *is swirling and floating around the dance floor in her full-skirted dress, with* ERROL *as her partner. She is wearing an orchid corsage.*

DOLLY: They're looking at us.

ERROL: That's 'cause you're the prettiest girl here.

DOLLY: I'm not sure …

ERROL: I am. You look a picture, Dolores. I said that.

DOLLY: You did.

ERROL: Well, you do. [*Teasing her*] And you haven't stepped on my toes once.

> DOLLY *slaps him on the arm gently and he grabs the hand and squeezes it tight. The song ends but he's still holding her hand tightly.*

DOLLY: They are looking at us. Nancy Woolthorpe, and the others.

ERROL: She's probably jealous. Not to be mean, but you look much nicer than she does.

> DOLLY *is nervously pleased with his boldness.*

Now, I'll get us a punch. Don't you go anywhere, now.

> *She just giggles.* ERROL *exits to get the drinks.*

> *The lights change for a dream sequence.*

COMPERE: [*voiceover on a squeaky microphone*] And the winner of the Miss Mooroopna-Shepparton Ball is … Miss Dolores Banks.

> *A sash is hung over* DOLLY's *shoulder.* DOLLY *is astounded—so excited.*

> *The lights snap back to reality.*

Repeating, our inaugural Miss Mooroopna-Shepparton is … Miss Nancy Woolthorpe. Could she step up, please … ?

> *Clapping and cheering can be heard.*

Isn't she a picture? Put your hands together for Nancy! The prettiest little gal in town.

> *But before she accepts the sash, we hear* NANCY WOOLTHORPE's *voice:*

NANCY WOOLTHORPE: [*voiceover*] Why, if it isn't Miss Dolores Banks herself. Love your dress, Dolly. Love the fabric. [*With a giggle*] My mother quite liked it too. When it was our sunroom curtains. But, you know, I thought we took them to the tip.

> DOLLY *is frozen in shame.*

DOLLY: [*to herself*] My ball gown? Courtesy of the town bloody tip?

COMPERE: [*voiceover*] And here she is! Our very own Miss Mooroopna-Shepparton!

> DOLLY *runs out, humiliated. The band sounds die away and night sounds take over. It is dark and a weak light shines on her from the hall. Her chest is heaving as she tries to hold in the tears. From the shadows comes a voice.*

COUSIN: [*offstage, slurring*] Hey, Dolores, come over here.

DOLLY: Pardon?

> *She wipes away a tear and tries to compose herself.*

I mean, what?

COUSIN: [*offstage*] Come over here, I said.

DOLLY: No.

COUSIN: [*offstage*] No? Think you're too good for us.

DOLLY: No. I don't—

COUSIN: [*offstage*] I think you do.

DOLLY: I don't—

COUSIN: [*offstage*] I reckon you need to be taught a lesson—

DOLLY: No—

> ERROL *arrives looking flustered, holding two cups of fruit punch.*

ERROL: Dolly? I've been looking all over for you. Can you believe it, that girl, in the horrible pink dress—?

COUSIN: [*offstage*] This your friend?

DOLLY: Please stop it, Leon—

COUSIN: [*offstage*] This who you step out with?

DOLLY: Leon—
ERROL: What's going on? Dolly?

> *There is a scuffle in the dark.*

DOLLY: Get your hands off me!
ERROL: Why, you don't treat a lady like that—
COUSIN: [*offstage*] She's no lady, she's just a little—

> *The big-band sound strikes up inside the hall. A drink goes flying, a punching sound, then another.* ERROL *staggers back into the weak light, holding his eye.* DOLLY *runs through the light, sobbing, her dress slightly ripped.*

[*Offstage, yelling*] See you later then, Doll—
ERROL: Dolly? Dolly?

> *But she's gone.*

SCENE TWELVE: STORM BREWING

GLADYS *is knitting up a storm while* NAN DEAR *crochets.* GLADYS *looks at her watch and smiles.*

GLADYS: She'll be having a lovely time.

> *But* NAN DEAR *has a sense of foreboding and* GLADYS *picks up on it.*

What is it?

> *She doesn't answer but goes outside with the kero lamp.*

NAN DEAR: Dolly? Dolly?

> *But the only reply is the rising wind that makes the kero lamp flicker and blow out.*

SCENE THIRTEEN: WATERS RISING

As the lights come up, DOLLY *is sobbing down by the river. After a time she hears a noise and is startled. Again she hears a sound and raises her fists to defend herself.*

ERROL: Whoa there, Dolly. It's me.
DOLLY: I knew that'd happen.

ERROL: It wasn't very nice—

DOLLY: Nice? You heard them. It'll never change … some things never do.

ERROL: Don't say that.

DOLLY: Especially around here.

ERROL: Please.

DOLLY: It's true.

ERROL: Please, Dolly … Let's just talk, can we? Please don't run away … If I have to try and follow you again, I'll really get lost—you know about my lousy sense of direction.

He's trying to jolly her. She can't help but smile through the tears.

DOLLY: I sure do.

ERROL: Ouch.

His eye is hurting.

DOLLY: Let me look at that. You have … an ocular contusion.

ERROL: A what?

DOLLY: A black eye, buddy.

She leads him closer to the river. She reaches in and retrieves something from the river, which she places against his eye.

ERROL: What's this? Some traditional Aboriginal method?

DOLLY: It's Aeroplane jelly.

ERROL: Whatever happened to a good steak—?

DOLLY: It's mutton flaps or this.

ERROL: And you keep it in the river?

DOLLY: You see any icebox up there?

ERROL: Oh.

DOLLY: Stay still!

ERROL: Yes, Nurse Dolly.

DOLLY: Nurse … Oh. The river's rising.

ERROL: Is it? Oh … your dress!

He sees the rip in it.

DOLLY: [*with a shrug*] Who cares? It's a stupid dress.

ERROL: It's … it's the prettiest dress I've ever seen. Though you could've worn a flour bag and you would've still been the prettiest girl in the room.

Beat.

DOLLY: Really?

ERROL: Really. You're my Miss Mooroopna-Shepparton.

He moves in more intimately. Beat.

DOLLY: Really?

ERROL: Yes, really … Ouch.

His eye is hurting.

Say, where did you learn to hook like that?

DOLLY: Thirty big brothers. Well, three blood brothers and twenty-seven boy cousins. Who are like brothers.

ERROL: Twenty-seven cousins, whew …

DOLLY *punches* ERROL*'s arm with one knuckle.*

DOLLY: Yep. That's only the boys.

ERROL: I've got three cousins that I only get to see once a year. Twenty-seven! Do you all get together at Christmas? I can't imagine how many pressies you have under the tree.

DOLLY *snorts.*

DOLLY: What tree?

Pause.

[*Wistfully*] It would be nice … to have a tree, and presents. Nancy Woolthorpe has this great big fake tree … Last year they wrapped the presents in red paper and green paper.

ERROL: Sounds like my mum. She's mad on all the trimmings. Glass baubles and fake snow …

DOLLY: I bet you have lots of presents, at your house?

ERROL: Piles! All wrapped up and tied with ribbons! With not a bow out of place.

Beat.

Bet you have more fun than we do, though. Your mum, your nan, your brothers, your cousins—

DOLLY: Aunties and uncles. And Papa Dear! We just have a singalong. We don't go much for presents. Except for Papa Dear. He always

brings me back something special. Something from one of his trips.
You know the church sent him to Western Australia?

ERROL: All that way?

DOLLY: They ask for him everywhere …! I'm talking too much …

ERROL: No, you're not … I like hearing about your life. Your family …
it's different from mine. My dad expects me to call him 'sir'.

DOLLY: Gee.

ERROL: And my mum … well, she has these funny ideas sometimes …
rather, my dad thinks they're funny ideas. Take this—she wants to get
a job. She says she's at home, with nothing to do but bake and dust—

DOLLY: Sounds like Nancy Woolthorpe's mum.

ERROL: —but he says she's too delicate to work. Your mum chops wood!
With an axe and all! And skins rabbits! It's like your family's from
another country or something.

DOLLY: We are.

Beat.

I can look after myself, you know.

ERROL: I know that—now. And it seems you can look after me, too.

DOLLY *giggles.*

DOLLY: But it was sweet. To come to my rescue like that.

ERROL: He called you names! Awful names!

DOLLY: He called you a gin jockey!

ERROL: [*indignantly*] I told him I never touch the stuff!

DOLLY *giggles then stops. The jelly is falling apart a little and*
ERROL *eats some off his fingers.*

Port wine. Want some?

DOLLY *starts to eat the jelly from his fingers.*

DOLLY: Port …

ERROL: … wine.

*They move closer, a kiss imminent. Celestial music is heard. But
then she moves away.*

What's wrong, Dolly?

DOLLY: I can't.

ERROL: Why?

DOLLY: Feel like getting coshed every time we step out together? Can't walk down the street holding hands for being called names? And what would your dad say if you took me home to meet him?

> ERROL *is lost in thought.* DOLLY *moves further away from him, as if to leave.*

ERROL: Dolly, I've got something to say. I want you to come away with me.

DOLLY: Away?

ERROL: Yes. To the city. We can get married. You could get a job. We can get a little flat. Wouldn't you like that? A sweet little flat with a balcony and a sitting room and a kitchen with a real stove and a new-fangled Kelvinator and water on tap … That'd have to be better than the river …

DOLLY: I'd have to leave the river …

ERROL: We could be near the seaside. Brighton's nice. It's not far from my parents …

DOLLY: I'd have to leave my family …

ERROL: Well, we could catch the train up once or twice a year. Or they could come down to visit. Though we could only afford a small flat, on my wage, so they couldn't stay over, but never mind.

DOLLY: You want me to leave here, for ever?

ERROL: I'm offering you a better life.

DOLLY: A better life?

ERROL: In the city there's department stores so big you could spend all day in them. Why, in the city there's even little restaurants you can eat spaghetti, just like in Italy.

DOLLY: Spaghetti?

ERROL: The point is, you could live in a real home, for the first time.

DOLLY: A real home?

ERROL: We could even save for wall-to-wall carpet … I want to spoil you. You deserve it. You deserve better.

DOLLY: Better?

ERROL: You're repeating everything—

DOLLY: I don't understand what you're saying—

ERROL: I'm offering you a future … our future, together.

DOLLY: But … a real home? A real home is where there are people looking out for each other.

Beat.

Do they do that in your home, in your family, Errol?

ERROL: Well …

DOLLY: [*to herself*] Don't matter if the floors are dirt. Don't matter one bit—

ERROL: [*demanding*] Hang on. Are you saying you'd rather live in a humpy by the river? When I'm promising you the world?

DOLLY: Your world. And you're just assuming that your world is better. But actually, when I think about it—when I think about that nasty Nancy—she has everything that opens and shuts. I'm not so sure it is better. I wouldn't trade places with her for anything. And as far as what you're offering … no thank you. This is my place. I'm staying right here with my mum and my nan.

ERROL: But, Dolly—

DOLLY: No, Errol. Our life isn't perfect, but like Nan says, it's ours. And you don't respect that. I'm sorry—

She goes to leave but he grabs her arm. She shakes him free.

Let go of me!

ERROL: I won't!

DOLLY: You have no right—

ERROL: Please … Dolly. I promised I'd walk you home. At least let me do that.

DOLLY: No. And don't follow me, this time.

Beat.

I can look after myself … remember?

Thunder, lightning. And she's gone into the shadows leaving him, bewildered and alone. Utterly crushed, he exits in the opposite direction. From the direction in which she's gone, we hear a sinister voice.

COUSIN: [*offstage*] Well, hello, Dolly … thought I'd catch up with you …

The lights go down, then half up.

SCENE FOURTEEN: THE FLOOD

Rain and thunder and lightning.

The humpy interior is pitch-dark apart from a flickering hurricane lamp way up high on the shelf. The two women are packing up their belongings.

NAN DEAR: Grab the flour, Glad, and the tea.

GLADYS: I have done this before, Mum. [*To herself*] Only about a thousand times.

> *They pack up and move things higher, calmly and deliberately.*

Wonder if it'll go as high as '51.

NAN DEAR: Hope not. Got too much to do. Don't want to wait three days for it to subside.

> *Beat.*

Are you sure she's … ?

GLADYS: Safe? He has the utility … Unless the water's already over the roads … I'm sure she'll be fine … She's sensible.

NAN DEAR: She's with a boy. That'll make her silly, not sensible.

GLADYS: [*crankily*] You want to have a go at me for letting her go with him, then come right out and say it. Don't take it out on the girl.

> NAN *is put out.* GLADYS *now focuses on the encyclopedias.*

NAN DEAR: I'm worried, that's all.

GLADYS: Then just say you're worried, rather than … all that other nonsense.

NAN DEAR: I'm worried.

GLADYS: [*softer*] Mum … don't worry. I'm sure she'll be … as right as rain.

> NAN *tries to convince herself that she's being a worry-wart.*

NAN DEAR: Yes. Right as rain.

> *But when there's a heavy knock at the door* NAN *reacts. A* JUNGI *(policeman) enters.*

Is it my granddaughter? Is she okay?

JUNGI: Granddaughter? No, ma'am. I'm here to help you up to the tip site.

GLADYS: She was in Shepp—

JUNGI: There's no getting through tonight. They'll evacuate her to the church. If you could grab just the essentials …

NAN struggles to lift her Singer sewing machine.

Ma'am? Is this essential?

NAN DEAR: It's a Singer!

She plonks it in the pram.

GLADYS: Could you give us a hand with the encyclopedia set, lad?

JUNGI: My orders are to move all people first, before we move property. Property can be replaced, after all.

GLADYS: Not this, it can't. [*To herself*] Not on a picker's wage. Gawd, we'd be living on Johnny cakes. [*Pleading*] Look, it's real important. For my daughter, see. Not for me, but for my daughter. Please.

JUNGI: Rightio … Now if you would just—

GLADYS: You'll make sure they're high and dry?

JUNGI: Yes. Let's get on with it.

> GLADYS *hoists the bag of food over her shoulder and rushes up to help* NAN DEAR *with the pram. The* JUNGI *shepherds them out of the humpy. A noise outside makes* GLADYS *alert.*

GLADYS: It's a banshee wailing.

> *Suddenly, a flash of lightning illuminates the statue-like figure of* DOLLY. *The sight of her makes* GLADYS *freeze, as if she's seen a ghost. But* NAN DEAR *runs towards her.*
>
> *The second verse of 'Que Sera, Sera' can be heard: 'Then I grew up and fell in love …'*
>
> DOLLY *pushes* NAN DEAR *aside and resolutely steps towards the humpy. But when she reaches the door the* JUNGI *puts his hand up.*

JUNGI: You can't go in there. We're evacuating.

> DOLLY *is looking down, shamefully, but still she defies him and goes to push past. He is astounded that someone would defy him and reaches to grab her arm. She half screams.*

DOLLY: [*lowly*] Don't touch me.

She steps inside the humpy.

GLADYS: [*panicking*] There's another family. Down here. With six children.

>*She points.*

Help them.

>*The* JUNGI *shrugs and starts to move off.* NAN DEAR *follows* GLADYS *back into the humpy. The* JUNGI, *looking around for somewhere to put the crate containing the encyclopedias, places them on the ground. He vanishes into the dark.*

>*The song continues: 'I asked my sweetheart, what lies ahead ...'*

>*Inside the humpy* GLADYS *and* NAN DEAR *whisper in private.* GLADYS *then approaches* DOLLY.

Dolly, what is it? Dolly, please?

>DOLLY *ignores them.* GLADYS *stands there helpless.*

Oh, my God. What has happened to you?

>*She wails like a banshee.*

>*Rain, thunder, darkness.*

>*Time passes.*

>*The waters rise.*

END OF ACT ONE

ACT TWO

SCENE ONE: AFTER THE FLOOD

Dawn finds GLADYS *outside the humpy. The water has drained away, but the devastation has been wrought. Everything is saturated and muddy.* GLADYS *is agitated.* NAN DEAR *leads* DOLLY *out onto a kero-tin seat that catches a ray of sunshine. She's still in the same dress, badly ripped and muddied. She's shell-shocked.* NAN DEAR *hands her a cup of billy tea.*

NAN DEAR: That was a bit of a struggle.

> GLADYS *looks anxious.*

To find dry wood.

GLADYS: And clean water.

> *They are trying to be light, but their hearts are heavy.*

NAN DEAR: At least the tea was dry, eh, Dolly?

> *But she doesn't answer.* GLADYS *has discovered the box of encyclopedias and she's distracted, so she hasn't listened to the others.* NAN DEAR *hands* GLADYS *a cup of tea.*

GLADYS: Least the tea was dry, eh?

> NAN DEAR *notices the encyclopedias.*

NAN DEAR: Oh, my … oh, Gladys …

> DOLLY *doesn't even register.*

Every one, Gladys? Every single one, ruined?

GLADYS: Never mind.

NAN DEAR: Never mind! They were your dream—

GLADYS: [*fiercely*] No! No! They're only possessions. And what do they matter? People is what matters.

> *They both look at* DOLLY. *Beat.*

NAN DEAR: I've been thinking … Gladys … If you still want to move to Rumbalara … It'd be better for the girl …

GLADYS: [*by rote*] She's not a girl.

They both know it.

[*Whispering to* NAN DEAR] Should we send word to Papa Dear?
NAN DEAR: [*whispering back*] I think … best not. It's women's business.

> *They look at each other in despair, barely able to hold it together.*
> *Just then* ERROL *appears with a determined look on his face.*

ERROL: Dolly, I'm sorry. I've come to beg your [forgiveness]—
NAN DEAR: You've got a cheek. Showing your face—
GLADYS: You're responsible? You did this?
ERROL: What?

> *He looks at her dishevelled state.*

Oh, my—Dolly, what happened—?
NAN DEAR: You get the hell—!
GLADYS: [*angrily*] Please leave. Now!
ERROL: But, Nan Dear, Gladys—
NAN DEAR: Don't you ever dare call me that—
ERROL: I would never—

Dalara Williams, Lily Shearer, Phoebe Grainer and Frederick Copperwaite in Darlinghurst Theatre Company's Rainbow's End, *2019 (Photo: Robert Catto)*

GLADYS: Are you leaving? Or do I have to—?

> GLADYS *reaches for the axe.* ERROL *stops and backs off.*

ERROL: [*devastated*] I thought you knew me.

GLADYS: I thought I did too.

> *The two women move to stand by* DOLLY*'s side, in unity. Devastated,* ERROL *turns and leaves. They watch him depart, still angry.*

NAN DEAR: If he ever shows his face—

DOLLY: It wasn't him.

> DOLLY *goes inside the humpy. The two women look at each other in shock.*
>
> *The lights down, then up to the sound of bulldozers.*

SCENE TWO: THE MOVE TO RUMBALARA

RADIO: [*voiceover*] From riverbank humpy to white house is quite a step. It will shortly become reality for the Aboriginal residents of the tin and canvas shanties. The ready-made concrete sections are rapidly being fitted into place. The neat, new, prefabricated house is the first nearly completed unit in a new group of ten. This is the most vigorous attempt yet to solve Aboriginal housing …

> NAN DEAR *and* GLADYS *hold their humble possessions as the sound of the bulldozers is heard. Their humpy disappears.*

GLADYS: It'll be wonderful, you'll see. Dolly'll love it. Just love it.

> *The sound of construction.*
>
> NAN DEAR *starts to cough (and coughs whenever she is in the house from now on).*
>
> *The lights go down, then come up on the new housing. It's concrete, small, white and featureless. It's anything but lovable.*

NAN DEAR: Not quite the 'new deal'.

GLADYS: No.

NAN DEAR: [*grimly*] I'll make curtains.

GLADYS: Yes, Mum. Thank you.

> *The lights go down.*

SCENE THREE: THE BROADCAST

The lights come up on DOLLY *who is peeling big dirty potatoes.*

RADIO: [*voiceover*] It's Australia's Amateur Hour … where we showcase Australia's most talented performers. Here's one of them now …

We hear a man playing a gumleaf.

GLADYS *enters and looks around conspiratorially.*

GLADYS: Nan's out? This came for you.

She holds a letter. No response from DOLLY.

Aren't you going to read it? It's from the bank.

DOLLY: If you know so much, you read it.

GLADYS: It's an opportunity.

DOLLY: It's an interview for a job I'm not going to get. And that you want, not me. [*To herself*] Why doesn't anyone ask what I want?

She flicks the station in frustration.

RADIO: [*voiceover*] … the historic broadcast of the Rodney Shire Council meeting. On the agenda is Aboriginal housing …

GLADYS *is momentarily distracted by the radio.*

GLADYS: Housing? [*To* DOLLY, *frustrated*] So you're just going to give up?

DOLLY: Yes.

GLADYS: Dolly, please—

DOLLY: [*bitterly*] Look at you, Mum. You go on about the things I should be doing. Why don't you fix your own house? If you know what I mean …

GLADYS *looks at her, and something snaps.*

GLADYS: Well! I'll show you!

NAN DEAR *enters, drawn by the raised voices.*

NAN DEAR: What's going on?

GLADYS *picks up her hat and handbag.*

Where you going now?

GLADYS: To fix my own house.

GLADYS *exits in a determined fashion.*

NAN DEAR: What?

A bicycle bell rings violently. NAN DEAR *looks out the window.*

She's got a bee in her bonnet about something.

She turns to DOLLY *suspiciously.*

What were you arguing about?

DOLLY: She wants me to go for that bank job.

NAN DEAR: You told her that's silly?

DOLLY: Of course. How will I ever get a job now?

NAN DEAR *just looks at her thoughtfully. There's a knock on the door.* NAN DEAR *marches up to the door, grabbing a jam tin on the way. She opens the door and the* RENT COLLECTOR *is standing there.*

NAN DEAR: Mr Coody.

RENT COLLECTOR: Mrs Dear.

Silently she hands him the money. He slowly and deliberately counts each coin, writes out a receipt and hands it to her. She takes the receipt and moves back inside. She joins DOLLY *and begins shelling peas into some newspaper as if nothing has happened. They work in companionable silence,* NAN DEAR *occasionally stopping to read the paper.*

NAN DEAR: Do you read this here page for children? It's called the Piccaninny's Page … Fancy calling it that?

DOLLY *shakes her head.* NAN DEAR *continues to read the paper.*

Says they've got this new powder that's 'guaranteed to turn your skin white'. Know a few folk who'd like to get their hands on that!

DOLLY: Nan, you never sit down and read.

NAN DEAR: [*whispering*] I can't in front of her.

DOLLY: [*whispering back*] She's not here [*loudly*] so just go and read it. For once. Gosh, Nan.

DOLLY *shoos her to the seat with the paper.* DOLLY *takes over shelling the peas. The music ends on the radio.*

RADIO ANNOUNCER: [*voiceover*] We resume our live broadcast of the
   Rodney Shire Council meeting …
COUNCILLOR 1: [*voiceover*] … on Crown Land. We bulldozed the shanties
   but they're creeping back. This housing problem is not going away.
   The lack of sanitation poses a serious risk to the good people of our
   town—
NAN DEAR: This rubbish!

   NAN DEAR *walks over to the radio* …

COUNCILLOR 2: [*voiceover*] Why can't an ablutions block be built out
   there?

   … *to turn it off, but just before she does she hears:*

GLADYS: [*voiceover*] Excuse me …

   NAN DEAR *stares at the radio.*

NAN DEAR: That's her.
DOLLY: What?
NAN DEAR: Shh!
COUNCILLOR 1: [*voiceover*] The night cart, for one, can't get access for
   part of the year due to the flooding—
GLADYS: [*voiceover*] If I could say something …
NAN DEAR: See!

   She points to the radio.

COUNCILLOR 2: [*voiceover*] Then build it at Daish's Paddock.
COUNCILLOR 1: [*voiceover*] That's out of the question.
GLADYS: [*voiceover*] Why so?
COUNCILLOR 1: [*voiceover*] Daish's is our town tip site, that serves
   the whole of our community, not just an itinerant minority, as the
   councillor for the West Ward well knows …

   There's a roar from outraged councillors.

GLADYS: [*voiceover*] Oi! Re the so-called 'housing problem', it is a
   housing problem because us Aboriginals—

   NAN DEAR *and* DOLLY *are getting very excited.*

CHAIRMAN: [*voiceover*] Madam …
DOLLY: They're calling her madam!
NAN DEAR: Shh!

GLADYS: [*voiceover*] —us Aboriginals are not welcome in the townships—

CHAIRMAN: [*voiceover*] Madam!

> GLADYS *needs to fight to be heard over the roars of the councillors.*

GLADYS: [*voiceover*] And apart from those concrete humpies that you built—call them houses?

CHAIRMAN: [*voiceover*] Order! I must insist—

GLADYS: [*voiceover*] And what about the other families? If you won't let us build our own houses on higher ground—

CHAIRMAN: [*voiceover*] The Chair does not recognise this—

GLADYS: [*voiceover*] —as if we choose to live on a floodplain—not realising that we need water too—to cook and to clean—

DOLLY: Go, Mum!

CHAIRMAN: [*voiceover*] There are protocols! If you read the rules—

GLADYS: [*voiceover*] Maybe you don't think we do wash—

CHAIRMAN: [*voiceover*] Eject this interloper—

GLADYS: [*voiceover*] I'm not an interloper—I belong here—this is my land!

CHAIRMAN: [*voiceover*] Madam, read the rules! Eject her!

CROWD: [*voiceover*] Hear! Hear!

GLADYS: [*voiceover*] I haven't finished. In fact I'm just starting re 'the housing problem' …

> *Her voice fades out as she is being led away.*

> NAN DEAR *picks up the radio and shakes it.*

NAN DEAR: Oh … schizenhausen!

DOLLY: What?

NAN DEAR: The bloody valve!

> DOLLY *is flabbergasted.*

Oh, don't look at me like that! As if you've never heard someone swear.

DOLLY: In German?

> NAN DEAR *shakes it off.*

NAN DEAR: But my daughter. My Gladys! Did you hear her?

> *She's practically hugging the radio, as if it were* GLADYS.

I didn't think you had it in you, daught. [*To* DOLLY] Did you?

DOLLY: Not really.

They dance a little jig around the radio as the lights fade.

SCENE FOUR: THE CONTRACT

ERROL *hurries up the track and is relieved to see* GLADYS—*in a similar scene to the first time he saw her, chopping wood—but this time outside the new Rumbalara housing.* ERROL *approaches her very tentatively.*

ERROL: Mrs Banks?

> GLADYS *turns around.*

GLADYS: Errol?
ERROL: Can I …?

> *He means 'approach'. She nods and when she puts down the axe he feels able to step forward.*

You're here now?
GLADYS: Yes.
ERROL: Took a bit to find you—
GLADYS: Why are you here, Errol?
ERROL: I'm sorry to bother you. It's about the—
GLADYS & ERROL: [*simultaneously*] Encyclopedias.
GLADYS: We … I … won't be needing them any more. All the shillings go into the meter box now.
ERROL: Isn't there any way … ?
GLADYS: No.
ERROL: Oh … Thing is, the contract. You signed it.
GLADYS: Yes.
ERROL: So you need to cancel it. You're not meant to be able to. But there are circumstances …
GLADYS: I have 'circumstances' all right.
ERROL: But it has to be done in writing.
GLADYS: Well, I can't, can I?

> *Beat.*

I can't.
ERROL: You mean, you can't write?
GLADYS: You're slow on the uptake, lad.

ERROL: I've never met anyone—

GLADYS: —that can't read and write?

ERROL: Yes.

GLADYS: Now you have.

ERROL: It's none of my business, Mrs Banks, but you're a smart lady.

Beat.

GLADYS: I'm sorry about last time, Errol. I wasn't so smart then. I treated you unfairly …

ERROL: I still don't understand … Dolly was so upset … I wished she could have heard me out …

Beat.

GLADYS: Thing is, I'm sorry.

ERROL: Thank you, Mrs Banks.

They're both awkward. He holds out his hand to shake on it.

Thing is, ma'am, the letter …

GLADYS: The letter.

ERROL: We still need to write this letter.

GLADYS: We?

ERROL: We.

So she nods and they both sit down on the kero tins. Resting a piece of paper on Errol's book, they start to compose a letter together, ERROL *writing it down.*

The song 'Catch a Falling Star' plays in the background.

GLADYS: Are you still up this way frequent, like?

ERROL: Still got half the alphabet to deliver.

GLADYS: Could I ask you a favour, Errol? I can't ask my mother—she works day and night. And Dolly's offered, but—

ERROL: How is Dolly?

GLADYS: She's … she's okay.

ERROL: Do you think she'd—?

GLADYS: No, Errol, she won't see you. I'm sure of that.

A beat while they think about Dolly, each with their own sorrows and regrets.

ERROL: The favour?

GLADYS: Could you teach me, Errol? See, we had a school and good teachers at Cummeragunja at one time, that's why Mum has such beautiful handwriting, but then the mission managers were terrible and it was all downhill, and I got sent off to work for a family. A family of six and a big house to look after—who had time for learning? Then I married Len and we were picking and along came the children, and then the war, and we were all so busy knitting for the war effort and I thought I'd get around to learning from someone but they were all … so busy.

ERROL: I had no idea … that any of that went on …

GLADYS: Then my darn pride got in the way—

ERROL: It'd be an honour, Mrs Banks.

GLADYS: It would … ? Thank you.

ERROL: Pleasure.

> *Beat.*

So she's—

GLADYS: She's changed. I am sorry, Errol.

ERROL: Then I'll have to change too. I'll prove to her I can. That I'm worthy of her.

> *He gets up, folds the letter into the envelope and licks it.*

GLADYS: You do that, Errol. You just do that.

> *The lights go down.*

SCENE FIVE: PAY THE RENT

Time passes.

The song 'Somewhere Over the Rainbow' plays.

As the lights come up, it is early morning, but already blindingly hot.
NAN DEAR *is cooking outside, just like she used to.*

DOLLY: [*offstage*] Morning, Nan.

NAN DEAR: One egg or two, Dolly love?

DOLLY: [*offstage*] How'd you know I felt like eggs? Three.

NAN DEAR: A serve of eggs is just what you need—

> *The* RENT COLLECTOR *is standing there.*

Mr Coody.

RENT COLLECTOR: Mrs Dear.

DOLLY: [*offstage*] Gawd, Nan, it's only just past seven and already it's stinking hot. Tonight I'll have to sleep on the roof like the others. Imagine me clambering up there—

> *She walks in, heavily pregnant, and stops dead when she sees the* RENT COLLECTOR *who looks with disdain at her body.*

RENT COLLECTOR: Your arrangements will need to be re-evaluated, with the impending new arrival. I'm not sure that the house is suitable for an extended family—

NAN DEAR: That's not of your concern.

> *She gets the eggs out of the basket.*

RENT COLLECTOR: It is very much of my concern. Everything to do with the habitation of this establishment is my concern.

NAN DEAR: This is Aboriginal Housing … [*under her breath*] not your own private kingdom.

> DOLLY *makes a sharp moan.*

Go in, Doll.

> NAN DEAR *passes over the rent book and the payment.*

Here's the rent. Please leave.

RENT COLLECTOR: And the person I saw just leaving?

NAN DEAR: The midwife.

RENT COLLECTOR: I should think the hospital is a more suitable place—

NAN DEAR: [*to herself*] And hospitals is where they take our babies away.

RENT COLLECTOR: You realise it is outside visiting hours? Given your obvious flouting of the rules, I think—

NAN DEAR: I don't care what you think! You and your visiting hours. Your rules. No singalongs after dark. Your spying. You, mister, can go to blazes! I'll give you 'one' …

> *She raises an egg as he turns.*

Two … Oh hell, three.

> *He runs.* NAN DEAR *chucks the eggs, one after the other, at his departing form.*

DOLLY: Nan! What would Papa Dear say?!

NAN DEAR: Well, Papa Dear is not here to hear, is he?

> DOLLY *gives* NAN DEAR *a hug.*

And sorry, love, just run out of eggs.

DOLLY: Not sure I felt like 'em anyway.

> DOLLY *looks vulnerable, sad.* NAN DEAR *looks away to hide her upset. She notices* DOLLY*'s school assignment, the family tree, pinned up on the wall above them.* DOLLY *follows* NAN DEAR*'s glance.*

I never did get to finish that. Now there'll be a new name to add to it. I was thinking Reg, or if it's a girl … Regina. What do you think?

NAN DEAR: After Papa Dear? He'll be thrilled.

DOLLY: Nan, there's something I need to tell you … about that night—

NAN DEAR: Hush …

> *Beat.*

DOLLY: But I'm worried —that I won't love it. Because of—

NAN DEAR: No matter how they come into the world, you still love 'em the same.

DOLLY: Even if—

NAN DEAR: Even if.

DOLLY: Nan. About that night, at the cork trees—

NAN DEAR: You don't need to say a thing. I was your age once, too. And I even became a mother too, when I was your age. Now that you're a woman, I can tell you.

> DOLLY *smiles—she's finally a woman in* NAN DEAR*'s eyes. But her smile is tinged with sadness.*

There was this lad—my father had given him some work splitting posts—work was scarce. So on this particular day, it was the day the Great War had been declared, and he was full of fightin' spirit—and the other kind, that comes in a flagon—this lad, I knew him, and I, well, I liked him, and I thought … At seventeen you have these silly dreams, even if he was a whitefella—

DOLLY: What? A whitefella?

NAN DEAR: Yes.

> *Beat.*

What I'm trying to say is … that I married Papa Dear after I was pregnant with Gladys.

DOLLY: [*not comprehending*] That's all right, Nan—you were just married in the bush way. Even if Papa Dear was a preacher.

NAN DEAR: No, Dolly—See, I was walking home, taking a short cut, and—and—and the lad—he took advantage of me …

DOLLY: What are you saying, Nan? Oh, Nan. Oh, Nan … not you …

NAN DEAR: Yes.

DOLLY: Not you, too, Nan.

> NAN DEAR *nods and they hold each other.*

NAN DEAR: And that's why I didn't want you to have anything to do with—

DOLLY: A white boy?

NAN DEAR: Yes.

DOLLY: But it wasn't a … [*white boy*]

NAN DEAR: I realise that … now.

DOLLY: And Errol would never do anything like that.

NAN DEAR: You were so angry with him.

DOLLY: He wanted to take me away. He didn't understand that I could never leave you. He thought he was some kind of knight in shining armour. And he wasn't.

> *Beat.*

NAN DEAR: Sometimes, you have to move on. Leave things behind … Even things you love.

> *Beat.*

DOLLY: [*softly*] He said he wanted to marry me.

NAN DEAR: You can't marry him.

DOLLY: I hardly think he'd marry me now—

NAN DEAR: Because the lad, on the day war was declared, his name was—

DOLLY: What does that matter now? That was then—

NAN DEAR: —his name was Clem Fisher.

DOLLY: Fisher?

NAN DEAR: Yes.

DOLLY: And Errol's a Fisher.

NAN DEAR: Yes.

DOLLY: And they could be … related? Ah … I see.

> *Now it's* NAN DEAR'*s turn to be anxious.*

NAN DEAR: I know you like that boy—

DOLLY: Oh, no, Nan. I mean, yes. But, no.

>   DOLLY *shakes her head. She knows it's impossible.*

NAN DEAR: More than like him? Maybe you even love him? Do you?

DOLLY: Nan, I'll respect you. I will. I promise.

NAN DEAR: I'm sorry.

DOLLY: Finito. That's it then. Que sera, sera. [*Beat.*] Please don't tell
Mum about the cork trees.

NAN DEAR: She has her suspicions.

DOLLY: Please.

>   NAN DEAR *nods.*

NAN DEAR. And you won't …?

DOLLY: Tell Mum? About Papa Dear? No.

NAN DEAR: Us Dears and our secrets, eh?

DOLLY: Yes.

>   *Beat.*

Where is Mum?

NAN DEAR: Extra shift.

DOLLY: What's she saving for this time?

NAN DEAR: A lemon layette from Trevaks.

DOLLY: But she could knit one.

NAN DEAR: You know Gladys, nothing like a bought one.

>   *They laugh.* DOLLY *strokes her tummy.*

DOLLY: Perhaps you're right, Nan … I feel I could love it …

NAN DEAR: Don't you know by now that I'm right about everything!

>   *They both laugh.*

Everything'll be fine. You'll see.

DOLLY: Yes, Nan. Yes, Nan.

>   DOLLY *leans against* NAN DEAR *and closes her eyes.*
>
>   *The lights go down.*

SCENE SIX: ERROL SPILLS THE BEANS

The lights come up on GLADYS *and* ERROL, *sitting on a park bench, with the Inspector's report.*

GLADYS: Anyway, I tried to say my bit at the Council meeting—

ERROL: That must have been something!

GLADYS: Well … it achieved nothing … Now everyone is cranky with me … The families for drawing attention to us … people in the street … even Papa Dear had heard about my 'radio moment'.

> *She sighs. Beat.*

ERROL: Oh! Mrs Banks, if you're interested, we have a bonus volume—

> *He passes her an encyclopedia.*

GLADYS: No, Errol. Thank you, but no.

> *He puts the book away.*

ERROL: That's okay, Mrs Banks.

GLADYS: Aunty … Anyway, I sure appreciate you taking the time, Errol.

ERROL: Don't mention it, Mrs—Aunty. You sure you wouldn't like to try something … ?

GLADYS: Easier? No. We'll continue with this. I'm interested to hear what he has to say about us … [*Reading, hesitatingly*] 'During September I visited with thirty families who were in permanent res … '

ERROL: Residence.

GLADYS: ' … residence, some at the site of the town tip, known as Daish's Paddock, but most on the banks of the Gool … '

ERROL: Goulburn.

GLADYS: Of course. 'Goulburn River. The san—it—ta—sanitation arrangements were as follows …'

> *She shakes her head and closes the report.*

I'll continue with that later.

ERROL: You're coming along nicely.

GLADYS: I get nervous in front of people.

> *Beat.*

Speaking of people … how is your family?

His face clouds over.

ERROL: My family? Same as always, I guess. And yours?

GLADYS: Nan Dear, she has these little turns sometimes. Doesn't like the new housing one bit. Can't say I blame her. Won't go to the doctor, of course. My father, Reginald Dear, is still preaching. I don't know where he gets the strength.

ERROL: I'd like to meet him one day.

GLADYS: You would?

ERROL: Yes. One day.

Pause.

And how is … ?

GLADYS: Dolly?

He nods.

She's …

ERROL: She's … ?

GLADYS: Errol, straight up, what are your feelings towards the girl?

ERROL: Well, I think she's real—

GLADYS: Pretty?

ERROL: Very pretty—she's a living doll—but she's also—

GLADYS: Clever.

ERROL: Clever? She's sharp as a tack. And she's—

GLADYS: Kind.

ERROL: Kind as, but in a way that's very—

GLADYS: Modest.

ERROL: Yes, modest. She doesn't have tickets on herself. I like that about her. And I really like that fact that Dolly is—

GLADYS: Straightforward. Tells you what she wants.

Beat.

ERROL: No. She's not. I'm never sure what she wants.

GLADYS: But that can't be! She's always blurting out things, she can't help it. She's a Dear, and us Dears are well known for being straight talkers. I always talk plain—and her grandfather, Papa Dear—why, not a more straight-talking man ever walked God's earth than my dear dad.

ERROL: Your 'dear' dad.

GLADYS: He is a dear—not just because he's my dad, but because of all the things he does to help our people.

Beat.

There is a public meeting, in Melbourne next week. He's raising the housing issue once again. Would you like to come along? And meet him?

ERROL: I'd like that.

GLADYS: Of course Dolly'll be there. Maybe you can talk. You know what I mean—far be it from me to put words in your mouth! And, Errol … ?

ERROL: Yes, Gladys?

GLADYS: Whatever she thinks, I think you're beaut.

ERROL: I think you're beaut, too.

He goes to shake hands with her, but she pulls him into a hug.

GLADYS: Thanks for spelling out your feelings towards the girl.

Dalara Williams, Lily Shearer, Phoebe Grainer, Frederick Copperwaite and Lincoln Vickery in Darlinghurst Theatre Company's Rainbow's End, *2019 (Photo: Robert Catto)*

ERROL: That's okay. I even like her snotty googles. She's—
GLADYS: Special. She is. I couldn't have put it better myself!

>   *The lights go down.*

SCENE SEVEN: THE PETITION

The lights come up on the interior of a draughty hall with the impression of rows of seats. The three women, in their Sunday best, are sitting facing the audience on a row of seats.

A finger tapping on a microphone can be heard over a loudspeaker accompanied by the squeal of feedback.

MAN ON MICROPHONE: [*voiceover*] Ladies and gentlemen, distinguished guests …
GLADYS: This is a big moment for Aboriginal people.
MAN ON MICROPHONE: [*voiceover*] This is a big moment for Aboriginal people …

>   *The women laugh.*

DOLLY: [*whispering*] You should be up there making the speech, Mum.
NAN DEAR: Gawd no, that's men's business.
DOLLY: Not always, Nan. What's women's business, anyway?
NAN DEAR: Family business, that's what.
DOLLY: [*whispering*] Keeping the secrets, you mean. [*To* GLADYS] I'm sorry, Mum, about the bank interview.
GLADYS: [*whispering*] Well, why didn't you tell me about the nursing? My girl, a nurse! On a scholarship and all!
DOLLY: There was nothing in writing. I couldn't.
GLADYS: Keeping secrets from your own mother! Fancy—you going all the way to Melbourne. You sure that's what you want?
DOLLY: I'm sure, Mum. And with Nan's help with Regina …

>   *They both look at the pram and smile.* ERROL *walks in and makes his way over to* GLADYS *who hasn't seen him yet.*

NAN DEAR: [*pushing her lips in* ERROL*'s direction*] What's he doing here?
GLADYS: I invited him.

>   GLADYS *welcomes* ERROL. *He sits down between her and* DOLLY *and peeks in the pram.*

ERROL: Hello, Dolly.

> DOLLY *looks down.* GLADYS *jumps into action.*

GLADYS: Come on, Mum, let's keep an eye out for Papa Dear.

NAN DEAR: But …

GLADYS: Mum … Papa Dear'll want to see you …

> *She practically drags a reluctant* NAN DEAR *away, leaving* DOLLY *and* ERROL *alone.*

ERROL: Your cousin's baby?

> DOLLY *isn't sure how to answer.*

'Course not. That was a little boy.

> DOLLY *arranges the blankets in the pram tenderly.* ERROL *looks searchingly at* DOLLY.

She's not …

DOLLY: [*nodding*] She is.

ERROL: Why didn't you tell me? Why didn't anyone tell me?

DOLLY: It's not your business.

ERROL: [*stiffly*] You're married then. Congratulations.

DOLLY: No need.

> *He looks at her hand. No ring. He thinks hard.*

ERROL: Nine, ten months ago. That would've been around—

DOLLY: Please—

ERROL: The flood. That's why—

DOLLY: Please.

ERROL: I'm so slow on the uptake. Damn. I'm an idiot. Damn.

> *Beat.*

Are you okay?

DOLLY: Yes. I'm okay.

ERROL: Are you sure? Is there anything I can do? Of course not—you can look after yourself.

DOLLY: Most of the time.

ERROL: Dolly, I'm sorry. For everything.

DOLLY: Yes. Me too.

MAN ON MICROPHONE: [*voiceover*] We're just waiting on Papa Dear to present this here petition to you all.

VOICE FROM THE CROWD: [*offstage*] Been waiting years!

Laughter from offstage.

ERROL: I had hoped we could talk. About the future.

DOLLY: The future's different now.

ERROL: Yes, it is ... I've changed, Dolly. I realise I was wrong. For example, I will come up here, if you want. Because, where you belong, and your family, is important. To you, and to me.

DOLLY: I'm going to Melbourne. To nurse.

ERROL: You are? That's ... great. Good on you. Nurse Dolly ...

Beat.

Dolly ...

DOLLY: Yes?

ERROL: Do you know what's in my heart?

DOLLY: Yes.

He searches her face but she is looking in the direction of NAN DEAR *who is returning in a purposeful manner,* GLADYS *making up the rear.*

I'm sorry ... as much as I ... I just can't ... I can't explain ... but I can't do ... this.

She means her and him.

ERROL: Are you sure? Really sure?

She nods.

Then I'll respect your decision ...

But the longing between them is palpable. He turns away from them.

And I wish you all the happiness in the world. You, and your lovely little daughter. And I hope we can at least be friends.

DOLLY: I'd ... like that.

ERROL *turns away from her, to hide his emotions.* NAN DEAR, *now beside* DOLLY, *suddenly looks faint.*

NAN DEAR: Oh ... I think it's too much for me.

She means Papa Dear's occasion. She sits down with a thud.

A glass of lemonade.

GLADYS: Quick, Dolly, go.

> DOLLY *jumps up to do as she's asked.*

NAN DEAR: No, I need her.

GLADYS: Okay, Mum.

> *She hurries away.* NAN DEAR *gestures for* DOLLY *to come closer. In the background we hear the assembly singing 'The Old Rugged Cross' very faintly.* DOLLY *looks at* NAN DEAR *expectantly, but* NAN DEAR *is unusually nervous.*

NAN DEAR: I need a powder.

DOLLY: [*sternly*] You're not pulling tricks on me?

NAN DEAR: No.

> *Realising it's serious,* DOLLY *goes to leave, but* NAN DEAR *grabs her arm.*

Dolly—that lad.

DOLLY: I told him, Nan. I told him we can never be together.

> *Beat.*

I'll go get the Bex … Will you be okay here with Errol, Nan, 'til I get back?

NAN DEAR: 'Spose. No way I'm going to fall off my perch in his company.

> DOLLY *steps away.* ERROL *steps up to* NAN DEAR.

ERROL: If you want, Mrs Dear, I could drive you to the hospital.

NAN DEAR: No hospitals. That's where you go to die.

ERROL: Perhaps you'd like to go home? The company utility's outside.

NAN DEAR: You'd do that? Drive an old woman home? To Mooroopna?

ERROL: Of course. Even to the river. The Murray—that's your place, isn't it?

NAN DEAR: [*staring at him*] Brought up to respect your elders, eh?

ERROL: Yes—just like Dolly.

> NAN DEAR*'s moved, but tries to hide it with gruffness.*

NAN DEAR: Fisher? What kind of fool name is that for someone who couldn't even gut a fish?

ERROL: I've never even caught a fish.

NAN DEAR: Thought not, your hands are too soft. What kind of man has soft hands?

> DOLLY *returns with a packet of Bex and a glass of water, but hangs back, curious. It's the first time she's seen* NAN DEAR *speak directly to* ERROL.

ERROL: Actually, ma'am, my dad changed our surname after the war. After they emigrated here. It was originally Vischer. But we Germans weren't the most popular. People used to throw stones at our house.

NAN DEAR: Oh? They did?

> *She almost seems happy to hear this. It dawns on her.*

So you're a fake Fisher?

ERROL: 'Fraid so.

NAN DEAR: Not even a real one?

ERROL: 'Fraid not.

NAN DEAR: Not related to any Fishers, even?

ERROL: No, ma'am.

> *It dawns on* DOLLY *and* NAN DEAR *simultaneously.*

DOLLY: That means …

NAN DEAR: Dear God. Thank goodness.

> NAN DEAR *reaches over and gives him a smacking kiss on the cheek.* DOLLY *stands there, agape.* GLADYS *rushes up with the glass of lemonade—she hasn't seen the kiss.*

GLADYS: Here's your lemonade, Mum.

NAN DEAR: You know I never touch that stuff. Bad for my sugars. Give it to Dolly.

> GLADYS *is completely exasperated. She has not yet noticed* DOLLY's *expression.*

WOMAN ON MICROPHONE: [*voiceover*] We can't wait much longer for your father.

GLADYS: He'll be here.

WOMAN ON MICROPHONE: [*voiceover*] Right you are …

> DOLLY's *baby cries and* GLADYS *turns her attention to the pram.*

She's speaking to DOLLY, *not even noticing the* DOLLY *and* NAN DEAR*'s sudden mood change.* ERROL *is just bewildered.*

GLADYS: Papa Dear will be here soon. I hope that you, Regina, will be as lucky as I am. Papa Dear … he's the best father a girl could ever have.

DOLLY: [*to* GLADYS] Mum, I've got something to tell you. Papa Dear's not—

The squeal of a microphone.

GLADYS: Not what? Not coming? 'Course he is!

DOLLY *hesitates.*

WOMAN ON MICROPHONE: [*voiceover*] Ah … we've just had word. Papa Dear's been caught up at a funeral. If Uncle Wally is here, can he present the petition? Where are you, Uncle?

GLADYS *stares in the direction of the voice, then something snaps.*

GLADYS: Petition. Uncle Wally … What's he got to do with this?

She marches up to the podium.

I will present the petition. [*Tremulously*] After all, me and my father Papa Dear, we came up with this here petition together … Gawd, I'm nervous— [*To an audience member*] Oh, hi there, Aunty …

She closes her eyes and without looking at the paper she begins.

As you know, William Cooper tried to present a petition to King George a few years back, but it was refused. Maybe our current monarch will listen to what we have to say.

Her Majesty, Queen Elizabeth the Second, Queen of England and her territories. We humbly present this petition to you … [*To herself*] Why humbly? We've been humble too long. Anyway …

She continues confidently.

We request … [*To herself*] No, we don't, sorry Papa. [*Continuing*] We demand to be heard.

CROWD: [*offstage*] Hear, hear.

GLADYS: Your Majesty, Queen Elizabeth the Second. We demand suitable housing for the Aboriginal people. [*To herself*] Yes, we got Rumbalara. And I'll be the first to admit, the idea sounded good. But—have you seen it? Concrete. No doors inside—so, we don't need privacy, not like regular folk, is that it? We want decent houses. Mrs Windsor, would you live at Rumbalara? Then why is it good enough for us? Why do we have to prove we can live like whitefellas, before we get the same opportunities? And, to boot, we're watched over like a bunch of cheeky kids … We're second-class citizens in our own country. No, we're not even citizens. Heavens, and this is the fifties!

We demand the right to control our own destiny. Now how exactly did Papa Dear word it … ?

She looks at the paper. She's lost her train of thought. She begins to panic. She's up in public, reading. She looks at the piece of paper wildly.

VOICE: [*offstage*] Do you need your glasses?

GLADYS: No.

There is a sustained moment of tension, then she hesitatingly reads one word, then another, then another.

'We demand the right to make our own decisions, and not be at the whim of government, at the mercy of Protection Boards, at the vagary of landlords and property owners.'

'We demand proper schooling.' [*To herself*] And not just for us. [*Continuing*] 'The white people too—they need to be educated about us, and our ways.'

She is reading more fluently now.

'Opportunities. We want jobs in town for our sons and daughters. We want them to go to universities.' [*To herself*] Yes! Not just high schools but universities! And why not? They say we can't learn, but we can. We can do anything once we set our minds to it, eh?

'We, the undersigned, demand to be the equal of anyone. And we will fight for that right. And keep fighting. Until we are treated right. By our neighbours and employers. By the Shire, by the Crown, by Mr Menzies.' [*To herself*] And if it's not him, then the next Prime Minister. Or the one after that.

Lastly, and this isn't in the petition, but maybe it should be, I don't want my mother to be served last in the butcher's. And I want townsfolk to say, 'Hello, lovely day'. Not cross the road to avoid us like we're lepers. [*To her audience*] We can get along with each other, can't we?

> ERROL *and* DOLLY *look at each other, longingly.* NAN DEAR, *as always, notices this and smiles.* GLADYS *has revved the crowd into a frenzy, but as she looks at them, she stops abruptly, her natural modesty reasserting itself.*

Goodness, I think I've said more than enough. But please, sign our petition. Come up to me afterwards. If you want me to read any part to you … I can. Thank you.

> GLADYS *ends her speech to tumultuous applause.* DOLLY *and* ERROL *again look at each other, very emotionally, clapping hard.*

VOICE: [*offstage, yelling*] That's the spirit. She's Papa Dear's daughter all right!

> GLADYS *joins her family, excitedly. They hug her.*

NAN DEAR: You done us all proud, Gladys. Your dad'd be …

> *A knowing look passes between* NAN DEAR *and* DOLLY.

… real proud of ya.

> *The baby makes a sound, as if she wants some of this attention.* ERROL *and* DOLLY *both automatically turn to the pram.*
>
> *The last verse of 'Que Sera, Sera' begins:*
>
> > *'Now I have children of my own …'*
>
> *The lights change for* NAN DEAR*'s dream sequence.*
>
> *Wedding bells and confetti as* DOLLY *and* ERROL—*pram in the middle—get hitched.*
>
> *The lights snap back to reality:*
>
> > *'They asked their mother, what will I be …'*

NAN DEAR: Oh, for heaven's sake! Dolly, marry this boy, before someone else does—I saw your cousin Pauline eyeing him off.

DOLLY: What? Are you sure?

GLADYS: Mum, are you sure?

ERROL: Are you really sure?

NAN DEAR: Yes! Yes! Of course I am. I can recognise a good man when I see one.

> 'Will I be handsome, will I be rich ...?'

> GLADYS *rolls her eyes, incredulous.* DOLLY *and* ERROL *hold each other's hands and look at each other adoringly.*

ERROL: Thank you, Mrs Dear, for your blessing, Mrs Dear.
NAN DEAR: It's 'Nan Dear' to you ... son.

> 'I tell them tenderly ...'

ERROL: Yes, Nan Dear.
DOLLY: And, Mum ...?
GLADYS: Yes, Dolly?
DOLLY: It'll be all right.
GLADYS: You always say that.

> *A commotion is heard in the background.*

DOLLY: It's Papa Dear! He's here! He's here!

> *The lights fade out on the 'Que Sera, Sera' chorus.*
> *'Que sera, sera,*
> *Whatever will be, will be,*
> *The future's not ours to see,*
> *Que sera, sera,*
> *What will be, will be,*
> *Que sera, sera ...'*

THE END

GLOSSARY

bodgies	boys who adopted certain fashions and behaviours during the 1950s
buka bung stew	stew made from nettles
goomees	drinkers
gubba	whitefella
humpy	a rough dwelling; a bush hut made from found materials
mamel	carpet snake
moom	bottom
widgies	female equivalent of the bodgies (see above)